The
Cheese Making
Book

By
Paul Peacock

Published by Farming Books and Videos 2007
Part of The Good Life Press Ltd.

ISBN 978 1904 871 24 8

A catalogue record for this book is available from
the British Library.

Published by
Farming Books and Videos
PO Box 536
Preston
PR2 9ZY
www.farmingbooksandvideos.com
www.thegoodlifepress.co.uk

Cover design and drawings by Firecatcher Books
Set by The Good Life Press Ltd.
Printed and bound in Great Britain by Cromwell Press.

The
Cheese Making
Book

By
Paul Peacock

Contents

Introduction Pages 9 - 14

Chapter One | A Cheesy Past 15 - 19

Chapter Two | The Dairy 20 - 28

Chapter Three | Milk and Moulds 29 - 37

Chapter Four | The Basic Principles 38 - 40

Chapter Five | The Science 41 - 49

Chapter Six | Your First Cheese 50 - 58

Chapter Seven | Further Techniques 59 - 66

Chapter Eight | When It All Goes Wrong 67 - 70

Chapter Nine | Thinking of Selling? 71 - 76

Chapter Ten | Showing Off 77 - 80

Chapter Eleven | Notes on the Recipes 81 - 85

Chapter Twelve | The Recipes 86 - 130

Appendix   Glossary 131 - 137
                  Resources 138 - 144

Mr. Peacock,

I have been told by Mr. H. G. Wells, who frequents my club in London, that you will be writing a book sometime in the century after next on cheese making. I am writing to ask if you would reconsider this disastrous action. I do not write because I hate cheese, or cheese makers for that matter, but on behalf of those with an artistic temperament and a keen nose everywhere.

I myself like cheese. It is noble in origins and a food fit for raising strong, healthy, intelligent and fecund children. Cheese is good for you.

However, it does hum a bit. If you cannot bring yourself to abandon this risky venture, you might consider asking people to start eating cheese out in the garden or in the public park. It is not ideal for what you will come to refer to as 'long car journeys,' whatever dreadful occurrences they may be, and should never, ever, be taken onto a railway carriage.

I should like to convey to you, by way of evidence, a report of a railway journey I undertook with a friend's cheeses. The carriage was hot and the cheeses were ripe. One lady looked at me uncomfortably and opened the windows. The cheeses had been bought from a disreputable gentleman in Liverpool and they were being transported to London on his behalf.

The lady got out of the train at the next station, complaining that it put her in mind of a dead baby and fairly soon I was left in the company of a sole tramp, who was asleep. Indeed, he woke at Crewe, spat out of the window and proceeded to rummage through his things, presumably to find whatever had died amongst them.

When I arrived at my friend's house his wife, a delicate lady with 'sensibilities,' decided to leave the house in the charge of the cook, taking their children with her. She embarked to a local hotel and wrote a note to her husband to the effect that she would not return until the cheeses had been consumed.

When he reckoned the cost of transport, the rent on a hotel room for his wife and her two children and the inflated price he had paid for the material in the first place, it had cost him a guinea an ounce. He declined to eat cheese after that, saying he couldn't afford it.

My sentiments entirely.

Yours Faithfully,

Jerome K. Jerome
London, August 1897

Introduction

"The bigger the dairymaid, the better the cheese."

There is nothing cheesy about cheese. The fact that you can take the contents of a calf's stomach and use it to make its mother's milk go sour and solid is one of the most wonderful transformations in the world. It was supposed to be Samuel Johnson who said, "He was a brave man who first ate an oyster." But one would think that he was a braver one who first made cheese. Actually, the making of cheese is not so gruesome and certainly opens the door to a world of wonderful flavours.

There are many reasons for making your own cheese. Of course the mantra of knowing exactly what is in your food applies to cheese as to anything else. When I was a child we used to buy cooking cheese from the grocer that would be sold today as extra mature cheddar. We have lost the ability to really know about the food we eat; we just take it for granted that a supermarket wouldn't dare sell a poor quality product. "There are laws about that, aren't there?" I heard a lady say in a shop once.

If you make your own cheese you will at least know most of what is in your food. You would have to buy organic milk to be completely sure that what you have on your cracker does not also contain a whole bunch of antibiotics, pesticides and cow hormones.

But as far as possible, within a retail system designed to maximize profits and to pretend to give us choice, you can have a product of which you are in control.

Secondly, you can make good and tasty cheese worthy of the name cheese. You can produce a product that is far better than you'd buy in the shop. Well, that's not quite true. Cheap cheese costs £4.50 a kilo as I write this, and you can make a product that would be as good as something costing three times this for around a fiver a kilo. (If you are reading this in the future, a dreadful time when we all belong to the state, you'll have to work the analogy out for yourself, if they have taught you to do that, and if owning books like this isn't illegal).

Thirdly, you will have acquired some skills. My great grandmother used to make cheese with a bit of lemon juice and some old milk and would drain it in muslin on the washing line and eat it on a slice of bread for her tea. (Tea is northern speak for the early evening meal!) Hands up how many of you have the skills to do that, even though it is a rudimentary part of every day food production.

You know you are a slave when you believe that the only way to make and enjoy cheese on some crusty bread is to buy it from the shop. The very basics of what keeps you alive is taken from your grasp. A loaf of bread and a piece of cheese; you do not even have to kill anything to make a cheese sandwich! When even this basic ability is taken away from you and you are forced, by lack of knowledge, to buy their pap and smear it with their cheese; you are indeed a slave.

As we have already hinted, cheese making is actually quite easy. It only requires a few household implements and is surprisingly successful. If you stick to the rules you will find it impossible to really mess up. One of the biggest barriers to making cheese is the idea that it is an industrial process. Surely you need lots and lots of milk! You must have special steel tanks and enormous amounts of refrigerated storage to mature the cheese because that's what people have seen on the television.

The answer to this is not so!

You can make a really good quantity of cheese with as little as two litres of milk and some lemon juice. You do not need anything more technical than your finger to measure the temperature (though a thermometer is probably more accurate), a cooker, a large pan and some cheesecloth. In around an hour you can make cottage cheese, not the runny stuff that they seem to sell as cottage cheese (though I do like it, it's not really cottage cheese), but a crumbly, loose association of moist but dryish curds that taste like the very best Cheshire cheese you could imagine.

Then, while you are eating your own creation, you can imagine how to augment this cheese, tasty though it is. Herbs, chives, sage, mint, garlic, bacon, pineapple, pepper; the wide range of soft cheese products on the market are now at your fingertips. (Although I love it, I haven't eaten Boursin for years, because I can make my own). Anyone can see that when you turn two litres of milk into a pound of cheese, economically you are on to a winner.

When I was a boy we ate cheese. It was cheese from a shop. Everything else was a horrible, inedible mess. French Cheese! No way! What I ate was cooking cheese, frequently hard and strong flavoured, it would sometimes make a salad or be toasted under the grill, or, best of all, melted on a tin plate over some grilled bacon and a little milk and mopped up with pieces of bread.

It never occurred to me that my favourite meal was messier and runnier than any French cheese at which I turned my nose up when Fanny Craddock showed it on the television.

But then, when I was old enough, I went across Manchester on the bus to my grandmother's who gave me Cheshire cheese sandwiches with onion on them and I was blown away. A different cheese that was good to eat. This had the makings of a journey, and in a way it became one, though it was many years before I could sit in a school staff room and join all the female teachers with a bit of salad and a tub of cottage cheese while the men ate chips and smoked Woodbines.

There are hundreds of cheeses from around the

world in the shops today. Some are very well known and we will be looking at making some of these in this book. However, there are some really strange ones out there, and also some strange uses for cheese.

Some cheese is used to build with and some extra mature cheese has been used in cement. A variety of cheese from Italy called casu marzu (rotten cheese) is a pecorino which has been infested with the larvae of flies which live in and eat the cheese and make it pungent, creamy and chunky in texture. (Now go and have a sit down and a glass of water!)

Cheesemaking evolved because without it people would have starved. Cheese isn't perfect. It may be gorgeous, fascinating and wholesome but it is not perfect. It is not the sort of food that you eat every day because, according to doctors and people who think they know, it contains a lot of fat and a lot of cholesterol. But in the past it was the ideal way of preserving milk, and it will continue to look after human kind even when industrial, mass market cheeses are just a distant memory.

Do not think that you can save a lot of money making cheese – you cannot. True, you can make top quality cheese that is a million times better than the stuff you get wrapped in plastic in the supermarket. It is true, however, that if you were going to buy an equivalent cheese it would cost a lot more and in this case you will save a lot of money.

Futhermore, if you have your own supply of milk, then you really ought to make cheese from it to maximise what you get from your animal. It should be your aim, as a smallholder, not to throw anything away. Indeed, even the spent whey can go to the pigs or the chickens or make bread after you have forced every bit of protein out of it.

All things considered, home cheesemaking is certainly not to be sniffed at!

Paul Peacock
Manchester 2007

Chapter One | A Cheesy Past

Whichever way you look at it, cheese is an ancient food, even though we do not know how cheese making actually started. Some stories tell of killing calves and gaining an understanding of what was happening in their stomachs. Other stories describe nomadic races who, carrying milk in animal skins, found it curdled and became sweet due to bacterial action.

Certainly the Egyptians were not the first to make cheese, but the Egyptian Priesthood was certainly the first bastion of cheese making. They considered it proof of their rank to make something solid come from a liquid and to preserve and remove the 'bad' portion from the milk, and in so doing to create a whole new food. With the Egyptians, cheese making attained cult status.

Cheese over three thousand five hundred years old has been found in the tombs of the Pharaohs (though there really is no need to mature your own cheese for this long) and the walls of the temples show how to make both cheese and butter.

It is, when you come to think of it, a remarkable thing that milk should be several foods in one and can provide everything that a mammal might need for its development. But cheese is actually much older than even Ancient Egypt.

The Mesopotamians, Babylonians, Assyrians, Ethiopians and Sudanese have their own unique methods of making cheese and dedicate herds of everything from cattle to buffalo and goats for the raw material. It was these people who first preserved cheese with salt and under oil, a practice we still see today in feta from Greece. (Here is something the Greeks didn't invent!)

Some say the goat was instrumental in the production of the Sahara desert because they probably ate everything in sight. Certainly the desertification of this land is in part due to the North African love of goat cheese, milk and meat. Other commentators say that goats are plentiful in Mediterranean Africa because they can survive quite happily from the kind of scrub that exists in that climate. Which ever is true, it is likely that goat milk has been used in cheese production at least as long as buffalo, and certainly longer than cow's milk.

Cheese making has followed mankind's wanderings so much that the only inhabited continents without a strong cheese making history are the Arctic areas of North America and Australia, where sheep and cheese did not arrive until the modern era. Although China does not have a history of cheese, the peripheral areas including Tibet, Nepal, Indonesia and Mongolia certainly do. The Bai and Sani tribes of China, in a minority as they are, make a cheese that is almost identical to Italian. For many centuries they have produced a cheese that is now known as the Mozzarella of the East.

It is said that the rich head of a village paid his workers in milk. One man, Zhang Zhi, mistakenly heated up some old milk and then added some fresh, only to find that the milk curdled. He scooped up the curds and pressed them between his fingers and then dried them. This would indicate that the Bai Chinese discovered cheese making quite by accident. It would be no leap of faith to realise that the South American queso blanco and Indian paneer were also each discovered independently.

Indian cheese, or paneer (which is a term that covers many forms of cheese), is still made all over the world by individuals for family consumption. This was once the state of affairs in Europe, where cottage cheese would be the equivalent. Alas, if you were to ask 100 people to make you a bowl of cottage cheese, perhaps only one of them would know how to do it. (Which is just as well because you only need half a brain to make it in the first place).

In the West, goat milk and, to a lesser extent sheep's milk, have continued to be made into rustic peasant cheeses until modern times. A cow produces so much more milk that you simply could not consume all the cheese yourself, and so, over time, local industries grew selling individual cheese types.

When Charlemagne, Emperor of the Franks, was given Brie in around the year 800 AD, he commanded that he should receive two cart loads a year by way of tax. It became known as "Fromage du roi" until they started cutting heads off in the revolution, when it changed to "Roi de fromage". (From the King's Cheese to The King of Cheeses). From this time local cheese makers vied for the patronage of local rulers and as a result different 'brands' of cheese were developed.

Most European cheese was named, more or less, after the place where it was made. A number of cheeses were also named after the method used to make them. The name Cheddar, for example, no longer comes from the Somerset town, but is named after the cheddaring process.

The locality of cheese making does have an impact on the flavour and texture of the cheese because there are interesting variations as to which bacteria and moulds fare well in one region over another. Similarly, the predominant dairy cattle in any one region will have a major impact on the taste and quality of its cheese.

Agriculture in England and France in the late Middle Ages was devastated by the Hundred Years War. Men were taken from the land and many farms went out of production. Food production came to a standstill and people survived largely on goat's cheese, the goat being an animal which is able to eek a productive life from the most meagre of diets. Consequently the wealth of these two nations suffered in relation to other European nations.

Goat's cheese has continued to be a favourite in France, though not so much in the UK, although it is gaining popularity thanks to the recent interest in local foods. Cheese making in the UK very much reinvented itself in the eighteenth century when most of our modern cheese varieties were developed, but many French cheeses are at least a thousand years older. Yet cheese making in the UK does indeed have a pedigree much older than the Roman invasion but sadly all the original recipes are long lost.

Chapter Two | The Dairy

The room where you make cheese should be special. Of course, it can be your kitchen but that introduces a number of problems associated with contamination. If you are going to use your kitchen you need to be able to get everything out of the way when you are making cheese and must satisfy yourself that all the surfaces can be sterilised. Many old farmhouses used to have a dairy which was usually a special room with a quarry tiled floor.

Inputs

The dairy should have at least four areas that are more or less mutually exclusive. The inputs area is a place to store milk, a creamer for creaming, a butter churn for, well, churning and a place for preparing starters and the inoculation of milk for use in cheese and yoghurt making.

The inputs area should also have room for filtering and separating milk. Fancy making some really special Brie with half cream half milk? (Believe me it is death-by-cheese-and-cracker!) Then a place to make cream with your own milk is going to be important for more than just butter.

Production

Production will constitute a separate area for producing cheeses, for heating large quantities of milk, for adding rennet and straining, cheddaring and draining, followed by pressing.

Here you will need a good sink and a cooker unless you intend to produce commercial cheese in which case you will have to install large vats with immersion heaters. The ability to hang cheeses in muslin to drain is important, as is somewhere to clean and sterilise your equipment, spoons, moulds and pots.

Maturing area

If you can get them, a set of slatted wooden shelves or metallic slatted shelves will be best for maturing cheeses. People have a separate room for this and if you can separate your maturation area from the production by a wall then all the better. Some small producers use a specially modified shed. I know one producer who uses an old truck and another who uses a container that would go on a ship.

The maturing area needs to cope with a temperature around 8 to 15ºC and varying humidity. If you are a hobby cheese maker this might present some difficulties because the needs of one cheese will interfere with the maturing of another. Any small farmers wishing to sell their own cheese will probably be best concentrating on a single variety and storing only one cheese type together.

You will need a hygrometer to check and maintain the humidity of the air in the storage and maturing area. Again, different cheeses will have different requirements.

Washing sink and clothing

Have a separate space for your washing and personal hygiene and use this place to store your aprons or overalls. The home cheese maker will certainly improve hygiene by using disposable plastic gloves that are discarded regularly. You will be surprised how frequently we touch our bodies and clothes when working in the kitchen and we routinely touch our faces and hair without even thinking about it. Making cheese is one activity where we are in constant danger of spreading dangerous organisms and the safety net of salting is not available to us because we rarely add more than 1% salt to cheese and it can take more than three times this amount to kill germs.

Equipping the Dairy

Pots

A large stock pot capable of holding at least a gallon of milk is the first prerequisite for home cheese making. You can get two and four gallon pots too that will just about fit on a domestic cooker, but you will have to remember that four gallons of milk weighs over sixty pounds and manipulating this amount of milk is not an easy matter. A farmyard dairy that produces cheese on a more commercial scale will also need draining systems made from stainless steel.

Cheese making leaves behind a lot of whey that can go down the sink but is better used to make other things, including more cheese. A method of saving whey in large containers will, at some time, be beneficial. It can be used in cooking - bread comes to mind - and it can also be be used in animal feed, even if it's only for the dog! You can also use whey to make ricotta.

Strainers

A series of strainers from domestic colanders to large plastic baskets will be useful. A plastic strainer that can be used to scoop curds will also be especially useful for ricotta and other cheeses.

Cheesecloth

Needless to say you need lots of muslin to filter curds from the whey. Strainers are not good enough by themselves. Cheesecloth should be used at least doubled over and should have been sterilised before use. You can use cheesecloth to drain cheese in a traditional way by tying it to the washing line. It can be washed, sterilised and used again. You can buy cheesecloth already cut from your usual supplier or, alternatively, seek out your local haberdasher or market stall and buy a couple of yards. Cut it into squares and then sterilise it.

You can also buy filtering bags which come in all different shapes and sizes to fit in pans and hang from hooks or taps.

Cheese iron

I have always wanted one of these! It is a tubular knife for cutting into cheeses so that you can taste them. You can also use it to show off too! They are actually quite cheap to buy but unless you are a large scale producer they are not really needed.

Towels

It is better to air dry and mature cheese on a sterile and absorbent material and there is nowhere better to do this than on sterilised towels.

Spoons and whisks

A series of different spoons, some slotted, some large with holes, large ladles, straining ladles and whisks are all important items of kit that you will find you need as your cheese making progresses.

A set of measuring spoons will be a helpful addition to your kitchen and will also be extremely quick at measuring out salt and other ingredients.

Knives

A cheese knife for cutting curds is useful but not essential. You can use a bread knife just as well. You will need a long blade which allows you to get to the bottom of the stockpot without having to put your hands into the liquid.

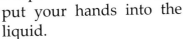

Thermometer

It is important that you are able to measure temperatures accurately. A long thermometer, preferably the bimetallic strip kind, will do and will make all the difference. Otherwise you will have to stir up the milk and take the temperature in two operations.

Resting boards

These are often wooden slabs. They are for letting cheeses such as Brie and Camembert rest. They are slotted and allow the mould to act while the cheese is still draining its whey, permitting the overall shape of the cheese to remain.

Cheese press

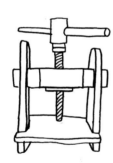

These are important. You need the associated moulds to go with them in which you will press your cheese. This has a number of functions. Firstly, it drives out the remaining whey from the solids. This is important because it contains a number of proteins and a lot of sugars. Whey is the portion of milk that goes off due to bacterial action and if you leave it in your cheese it will quickly become rancid, even if you have salted it.

You can make your own cheese press. A simple 'G' clamp will extract a large amount of whey from the cheese and produce a block that will easily crumble or spread. It is certainly sufficient for small home made batches of Cheshire type cheeses.

The Dutch press is fashioned from three pieces

of wood with a long handle from which you can hang weights which has a loosely fitted arm that is pushed down onto the cheese mould.

Heavy-duty presses have a greater pressing force that removes a greater amount of whey and creates a cheese that is more solid and ready for maturing into hard blocks. These are worth purchasing if you are going to create a lot of cheese. You could double up by using a fruit press, perhaps also using it for crushing fruit and making wine. Perhaps this is the origins of the cheese and wine party!

The moulds have an inner fitting plunger that you fit into the press and the basket is filled with holes, if indeed anything can be filled with holes! You have to line the basket with a double layer of cheesecloth and then press the cheese inside this. You will end up with a brick of cheese that must be removed from the cheesecloth because it will be rich in whey and will most likely spoil the cheese.

The environment for cheese making

Making cheese would not be allowed in schools because regulations control the growing of unknown organisms in a culture. You simply do not know what microbes are growing when you culture anything. Hopefully, everything is under control and your cheese contains nothing in it but what is supposed to be there.

For this reason it is important to maintain a

scrupulously clean room for making cheese. If you are planning on selling cheese you will need a specially designed room for your production and storage, but we shall look into this later.

In the home, everything should be sterilised including utensils and pans, cheesecloth, towels, sinks and work surfaces. However, some cheese needs to mature for a long time in a controlled environment. This maturation can both affect and be affected by other foodstuffs making it a potentially dangerous process so I mature my cheeses inside a large plastic box with a sealable lid. You can change the air in the box frequently but, more importantly, you can also sterilise the box itself and line it with a sterile towel to ensure the process occurs safely.

Before making cheese, sterilise all your utensils and pans. Boiling water in them for ten minutes will be enough to do this. Similarly, cheesecloth, knives and thermometers as well as press moulds need to be boiled. I prefer this to using chemicals, particularly on cheesecloth which will be significantly weakened. by disinfectants. You will need a constant supply of cheesecloth because boiling wears them out too.

Chapter Three | Milk & Moulds

Milk is marvellous, the stuff that heroes are made from. In fact, all mammals are made from it, more or less. So far as cheese making is concerned the fat content of milk is what largely makes the difference in flavour. For example, it is possible to make cheese from skimmed and semi-skimmed milk, but you will find full cream milk much better.

Moreover, the creamier the milk, the creamier the final product, and with this in mind sheep's cheese is by far the creamiest. Then goat's cheese and finally cheesemade from cows' milk.

(If I might be allowed a digression, the good Lord has provided us with a marvellous beast that will compete for your affections, even with the most beautiful of women. The Jersey cow has a little place for you to put your head while you milk her. She has beautiful eyes and the creamiest milk of all her kind. It is worth giving up a life of freedom and foreign holidays just for a single bucket full of her milk. So if you can buy yourself one, or get a regular supply of her milk, then you're on to a winner.)

Around the world people also make cheese using the milk of both yak and camel. Milk still has the same basic constituents irrespective of its source.

Protein

There are a number of proteins in cheese. Casein is the major portion and is not soluble in water. In milk it is held in suspension, a little like emulsion paint. It is not curdled by heat, by acidity or by the action of an enzyme such as those found in rennet. Casein translates as cheese, and is its major single constituent.

There are some water-soluble proteins that remain in the whey. They are often referred to as whey proteins, and these are precipitated by heat. They are used in the production of ricotta cheese.

Sugar

The major sugar found in milk is lactose, and this is left in the whey after the curds have been taken. It gives a sweet flavour to the whey and is useful in cake making.

Fat

The higher the fat, the creamier the milk and therefore the more flavoursome the cheese.

Minerals

Milk contains important minerals, often placed there to the detriment of the mother. These minerals are largely retained in the cheese, some of them by means of protein coagulation and the chemistry of lipids as they solidify. Cheese is a consistently good source of minerals.

Microbes

We have already said that the udder is full of bacteria, mostly 'friendly' (as opposed to 'polite') bacteria, but it has to be said that there are some unfriendly ones in there too. Lysteria is one such organism. Many people believe it is an inherent by-product of the cheese making process for certain soft cheeses and shun them for this reason.

People who believe in raw milk cheese making point out that the pasteurisation process destroys nutrients and changes the fat so that it is more likely to escape in the production process. They also reckon that the final product is not so easily digestible. On the other hand the opposing camp, mainly doctors, point out the dangers of Lysteria and its associated diseases, particularly for pregnant women.

Unless otherwise stated, the recipes in this book have been produced using pasteurised milk. All I can say is that in my opinion you can make some fantastic cheeses from such milk. I have a number of reasons in mind. We do not live in a Smallholder's Utopia where cream is made from clouds and milk comes from God above. For most people the supply of milk is uncertain and the pasteurisation process is therefore a small price to pay for the extra security. Some milk enters the country from abroad and I for one would be happier making cheese from these sources with pasteurised milk rather than raw.

If I had my own supply of milk for which I was responsible, and had first hand knowledge of the regime under which the milk was produced, then maybe I would be happy to make raw milk cheese.

I have been in a fair few milking parlours in my time, some of which you could eat your dinner off the floor (if you don't mind cow pat sandwiches). Others have been less scrupulous, and I would think twice about using this milk raw. Perhaps I'm a bit squeamish, but you have also to remember why pasteurisation was introduced; to increase the lasting qualities of milk without too much of a flavour change, and to drastically cut down disease from the numerous unsanitary milk parlours.

All that said, pasteurising does alter the protein and fat components of milk. When making cheese from pasteurised milk you will find that the curd is somewhat stickier and not as robust as when using raw milk. This is more pronounced the higher the fat content of the milk. As with everything else in life, you get what you pay for.

How to pasteurise milk

You will need a double boiler and a good thermometer. Slowly heat the milk to 66ºC and keep it at this temperature for 30 minutes. This is probably best achieved by turning the heat down on the boiler after ten minutes and then turning it off altogether, allowing the whole apparatus to cool naturally.

When the milk has cooled to the required temperature for cheese making you can use it immediately.

Organic / non organic

The best milk for cheese making is organic because it does not contain any antibiotics that will hinder the progress of the starter. There are legal limits to antibiotic content of milk, but from time to time they do cause problems. Milk bought from the supermarket comes from all over the continent (or even the globe!) as well as from the UK, and so, apart from the environmental ethics of food miles, you might not be happy using milk that has been produced under a regime you know nothing about.

If you have your own milk

It is very easy to taint your milk when you are milking your own animal. These taints can come from the animal itself if it is unwell, or from its feed or from the handling of the milk once it has been taken to the dairy. You need to be completely sure there are no taints in the milk because they will certainly be magnified in your final product.

You also need to be sure the milk is stored in a place away from other foods so, dependent on your ambitions, you may need a separate dairy where no other foods are stored. This is certainly the case when it comes to onions and garlic. If you are making cheese like a "roule" with garlic in it you will find it difficult to get rid of all the flavour and you may seem to be smelling garlic for ages.

Of course, if your animal is sick then the milk should not be used. If it is stringy or has clots in it then your animal probably has mastitis and you should discard its milk. Too high a bacterial content can also occur if the animal has not been cleaned properly following birth, and this will also present other symptoms.

Moulds

Cheese is associated with mould. I must confess that the idea of eating something mouldy goes against the grain. We also have to realise that cheese is hardly preserved at all, in the normal sense of the word as we would use it to describe cured meat. There is salt but it only forms 1% of the total weight of the cheese. We normally preserve meat and fish using much higher salt levels than this.

When moulds grow in the cheese they produce all kinds of chemical inhibitors that stop other moulds and, most certainly, bacteria from growing. If we make sure there are no other contaminants, both bacterial and fungal in the milk, and add those that we know will do us no harm, then the cheese will benefit in many ways.

Remember that cheese is a food, and microbes grow well on food, but their action is somewhat inhibited by the moulds we add ourselves. The cheese is partially preserved by the moulds we have added and the fact that by doing so we have kept the other germs out.

Of course, over time any cheese will become prey to the attentions of spoiling bacteria, but it is usually consumed before this can happen. Other factors which help to preserve the cheese include the concentrated protein being difficult to digest by microbes, the high fat content, the air tight covering of a waxed cheese, the acidity, which is often around pH4, and the contribution of the salt content.

Cheeses that mature for longer than six months are protected by a hard rind and cheeses such as Parmesan which are almost (but not quite) dry, present a very difficult surface for any spoiling organisms to digest.

The moulds we add are:

Penicillium candidum
Penicillium roqueforti
Geotrichum candidum
Penicillium camemberti

There are two moulds in general use and these are blue and white. The white moulds work on the cheese from the inside to eventually create a soft, runny cheese. They are creamier and spread easily. Blue moulds are mostly found in harder cheeses and add a bitter, more acidic flavour and, when ripe, some would say an amoniacal flavour to the cheese.

Blue moulds

These are produced by adding a culture of Penicillium roqueforti to the cheese at the starter stage which is accelerated later in the maturing stage when air is introduced by a skewer or needle. This causes the cheese bacteria to create the blue colour and also the change in texture and flavour. In order to mature well these cheeses need a high humidity, around 90%, and achieving this without at the same time having a hot room is not easy.

You can buy Penicillium roqueforti in sachets that will keep in the freezer. A single sachet will be enough for 250 litres of milk, so if you are creating only small amounts of cheese you will have to be careful on two fronts. Firstly, that it is frozen well and secondly, that you do not introduce any other organisms into the sachet when you are producing the cheese.

White moulds

These are produced by the action of Penicillium candidum, inoculated at the starter stage or the maturing stage. The starter stage is easier to do for the home cheesemaker because it is less messy. Spraying a culture of Penicillium candidum from a household spray onto the cheese means having to completely sterilise a complex piece of equipment. This is normally done by filling it with Milton solution and spraying it through the nozzle. Then wash the whole thing out in the same way by spraying cooled boiled water through it. (Otherwise you would kill your precious mould spores).

Penicillium candidum comes in sachets in the same way as Penicillium roqueforti.

Chapter Four | The Basic Principles

Casein is a protein that will go rock hard in the presence of acid. So hard, in fact, that during World War One soldiers' uniforms were in effect made out of milk which was ironically supplied by Germany.

If you add acid to milk it will precipitate at pH4.6 and the sweet smelling lactic slurry that results can be strained, pressed and moulded into anything, including buttons.

This is the basic principle of cheese making. Casein is a protein that is made up of straight chains of molecules, held together by phosphates and when you acidify this material, it coagulates. And that is really all there is to it.

To coagulate the molecule you can add acid, as we have already stated. This can be in the form of lemon juice, which is an accepted procedure as we will see later. A more subtle way, and possibly the way the very earliest cheese was made, is to allow the natural bacteria in milk to reproduce and release their own acid – lactic acid. Once the pH level has reached 4.6 the curds will begin to form.

A totally different way of coagulating the protein is to knock off the phosphates, and this can be done chemically by the addition of a coagulating agent or setter. Rennet is a digestive protein that does just that. You can also find chemicals in nature that will do the same job but which do not come from an animal's stomach.

The coagulation of milk protein is the first fundamental of cheese making but there is much more to it than that. You must remove all traces of the sugary residue that is left behind as the curds form. This whey should not be wasted, but can be fed to pigs. It is nutritious and is simply the constituent part of milk that goes off easily. Once removed, the curds can be collected together and salted to preserve the cheese.

The problem is that when you do salt, more then comes out, so the production of simple un-pressed cottage cheese is a fine balance between salting and washing.

Then the cheese can be pressed and cooked in

various ways to create a solid block, or layered to create a soft cheese that runs. Finally, the cheese can be matured, and here you are growing bacteria and mould that concentrates the flavours and creates a special type of cheese.

Subtler still, the temperature at which the curds are coaxed out of suspension in the milk can have a dramatic effect on the final flavour of the cheese, as can the acidity. Milk is frequently inoculated with a special blend of bacteria to increase its acidity in a natural way. After this the same bacteria grow in the cheese and create a special blend of texture and flavour.

This book presents several options for making your own cheese. Firstly, there is the staple cheese that you would use in cooking. Four litres of milk will make half a kilo of cheese in just a couple of hours. This will be suitable for adding to any dish you care to mention. This sounds a lot, but if you are thinking of getting or already have your own cow, then you'll be making a lot more than this! Secondly, there is the speciality cheese that makes life heaven. To make your own Brie (although if you happen to live just outside Cleethorpes you may be barred from calling it Brie!), is the most wonderful thrill in the world. And finally, because some people are allegeric to cows' milk but can tolerate goat and sheep milk, we also include some delicious recipes using these as well.

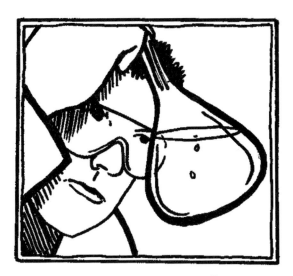

Chapter Five | The Science

Cheese is made by the action of acid on casein, or the action of an enzyme on casein, or both. There are important reasons for this distinction. Simple cheese can be made by adding lemon juice to milk. It doesn't last that long, it's not over creamy, but is quick and simple. Adding a culture of bacteria to the cheese increases the acidity and after a while the milk will curd of its own accord. The yield would be low, but the cheese would be much creamier. The use of a culture and the enzyme rennet makes a high yielding cheese which will be creamier and will continue to mature after the curds have been washed, salted and pressed.

Cultures and starters

Starter cultures are bacteria that give off lactic acid

as a waste product. This acidification, or souring process, can take around an hour or more and is often temperature sensitive.

Some cultures are better at around 40–44°C and are called mesophilic cultures. Others are more active at 50°C and are called thermophilic cultures. Mesophilic cultures are usually used for soft cheeses and thermophilic are used in some hard cheeses, although this is by no means a completely hard and fast rule.

The main point about cultures is that they provide the bacteria that will mature the cheese after the physical processes of creating the curds and pressing out the whey. The difference between many cheese types is basically down to the starter cultures that are used.

You can buy starter cultures containing exactly the right combinations of the specific bacteria and fungi needed to make the final product. In general, it is best to use these purchased starters because you will then be totally sure that your cheese will not contain any unplanned for nasties.

Another important consideration when it comes to starters is that they produce substances in the cheese that improve its keeping qualities. Cheese is not preserved solely by salt but by its acidic nature. This is particularly true of Cheddar cheese which needs a rapid build up of acidity in its production. One of the secondary characteristics of cheese, its texture, firmness and colour, are all also produced by the action of the starter culture.

Of course the creaminess of the final product, too, is also a function of the starter culture, partly because of the way the microbes attack the remaining sugars and fats and where their products dissolve. The microbiology of cheese is a complex business, the understanding of which, thankfully, is not a prerequisite for making good cheese.

Making your own culture

Culture is alive; a mix of various bacteria and milk that is constantly fed and grown by new additions of milk. Some dairies have had a culture going for many decades and their ingredients are top secret.

John Seymour's starter

John Seymour, the writer of many books on self-sufficiency including the great Complete Book of Self-Sufficiency, said he made cheese but it was more likely Sally, his first wife, who did the making.

Anyway, John's culture was simply the second quart of milk from the cow, allowed to stand overnight. This was then skimmed off and the cream given to the cat. What was left was then mixed with another quart of cooled pasteurised milk. Every day half of this could be used as a starter and half added to another quart of milk. In this way the culture was kept going for quite some time.

It is best not to keep starters for too long at home because you are bound to introduce all sorts of bacteria into the mix. It is well nigh impossible, for example, to keep Staphylococcus bacteria out of the mix and every time you have a piece of cheese you will get a sore throat. Large commercial dairies are able to keep starters under conditions that keep them pure. This is not possible in the home.

Buying a ready made starter

There are a number of starters that you simply buy in sachet form. They are freeze dried and last for ages. They do not need inoculating and are added directly to the milk before you rennet the mixture.

You can buy starters for all kinds of cheese and if you want to try your hand at Brie and Camembert then you need Penicillium candidum, which is added to the starter or washed on to the outside of the cheese when it is ripening. The hard white crust on the cheese is the Penicillium candidum that matures it from the outside inwards. Commercial Brie and Camembert manufacturers walk around the shelves of ripening cheeses with a spray of Penicillium candidum that washes over them. I am fairly sure this is not really necessary at home. For the making of blue cheese Penicillium roqueforti is also available in sachets.

If you are going to make a cheese like Cheddar and need a similar consistency and quality time and again, then you need to make sure you have your starter right. In this case it would be advisable to buy in a commercially available product.

MA400 is the basic all round starter that you can use for most types of cheese. It usually comes in sachets and you add it to a little milk to then inoculate your cheese. You can also buy it in a form that is simply sprinkled into the milk, stirred up and then left to do its job. MA400 is mesophilic and consequently does not need to be overheated.

You can buy specific starters for making different cheeses. Emmental starter is thermophilic and is a culture of Propionbacteria shermanii, which is responsible for the holes and specific flavour of this hard cheese. You can also buy specific starters for mozzarella and Parmesan.

Making up the starter

It's a bit of a cheat, buying a book that says 'read the packet', but that is certainly the best advice. Starters are individual products and have their own special requirements. Some will come with rennet included so you will have to read the label! (Don't say we didn't warn you!)

Making up an incubational starter is easy. All you need is the starter and some sterile containers. I have found a yoghurt maker to be ideal. Heat up some milk to nearly boiling for around ten minutes. In fact it doesn't really matter if you do boil it.

Transfer it to the sterile container (not forgetting to sterilise the lid!) and allow it to cool to room temperature. Add the specified starter (after reading the label!) and let it work at room temperature for 24 hours. It should then resemble a thick, lumpy, clean smelling yoghurt. It should also have a definite acidic aroma.

A sachet of starter probably contains sufficient for 250 litres of milk. You only need the tip of a teaspoon or 1g to inoculate enough milk to make a starter solution.

Sterile technique

As we have said, if you continue to reuse culture for a long period you will eventually introduce some bug that will do you no good at all. If you can (AND DO BE CAREFUL!), pour cultures from one receptacle to another over a candle or a spirit burner. Also, wear overalls when making cheese – even a hat!

Use Milton to clean surfaces and boiling water for knives and other utensils. The oven is the best way to sterilise glassware, but if you are using Kilner Jars, watch for the seal; they do collect bacteria and also deteriorate when overheated.

One of the most important places to sterilise is the kitchen sink. Because there is little room in the domestic kitchen, people tend to drain their curds in a colander in the sink. This can introduce all sorts of nasties into your cheese from soap to salmonella.

Alternatives to starters

You can make a cheese for immediate consumption without a starter. It will not mature and will not last very well, but at the same time it is perfectly acceptable as a rough cheese.

Both crème fraiche and fromage frais make effective starters, especially for cheeses that resemble creamy Lancashire. Natural yoghurt will also do the job, but make sure there are no seeds in it!

A lot of people use old milk as a starter. This is fine as long as you are completely sure of the health of your milk. Those people with their own animals should maintain their health as scrupulously as possible, and the milk should be tested regularly, especially if the cheese is to be used commercially.

About rennet

If you cut open a calf's stomach, an unpleasant and unfriendly thing to do at the best of times, you will find the milk that it suckled from its mother was all in a lump. The milk would be coagulated by the combined action of the acidity of the stomach and an enzyme that all mammals have called rennin. You may also find it occasionally called chymosin.

Rennin, like all enzymes, does its bit of clever

chemistry so that at the end of the process the rennin molecule is released intact, so that it can go and find another bit of milk protein and start all over again. This makes rennin, and all enzymes, a catalyst.

It is likely that the first cheeses were made simply by allowing milk to sour naturally but not to go bad as such. The resulting curds were then taken from the smelly mess of whey and solidified. It wasn't until a proper understanding of butchery that people were able to emulate the action of the calf's stomach, and this type of cheese became associated with sacrifice – popularised by the Egyptians.

Rennet is still made from calves' stomachs. Adult cows do not have this protein, so it must be a calf or a bull. This is one reason why some people decide not to eat cheese, some through a vegetarian ideal and others due to the fact that rennet comes solely from the young calf!

Vegetarian rennet

This is made from other chemicals that do the same job as rennet from a calf. In the past, rennet substitutes have been made from fig leaves, Lady's bedstraw, wild thistle and melon. They were not as efficient as authentic rennet, and for this reason most people still prefer the animal type.

However, a better vegetarian rennet is made by fermenting the fungus Mucor miehei or by using a rennet from the bacteria Bacillus subtilis or Bacillus prodigiosum. These sources produce a great alternative to rennet and you would be hard pushed to tell the difference between them and the old-fashioned animal rennet.

Genetic engineering has also produced a novel way of making real animal rennet. The DNA for encoding rennin has been introduced into some bacteria and switched so they produce commercial quantities of rennet. This substance is identical to the original animal product, but it doesn't need the killing of any calves. This source is increasing in popularity and was first commercially produced in 1990 and will continue to produce rennet more cheaply in the long run. In fact, it is about a tenth of the price to produce but this is not reflected by prices in the shops.

This genetically produced rennet, although not requiring the slaughter of any calves, will still not be acceptable to vegetarians. If this is an important consideration, all you need to do is to stipulate your requirement for vegetarian rennet when you are buying your supplies.

Chapter Six | Your First Cheese

In this section we will look at the very basics of cheese production and make a cheese that you can repeat time and again with little hassle. It will press into a reasonable cheese for the table. It will be a bit crumbly, but it will also make a fantastic soft cheese. This is a perfect base for adding all kinds of materials to your cheese and you could spend a whole year simply using this recipe and exploring its numerous possibilities.

A quick note: cheese making is not quite like any cooking you may have done before and it is a little counter-intuitive. For example, if you are making a sponge cake you pretty much know the quantities and consistencies you need. But when making cheese it is all a bit different. Our own first cheeses had a strange flavour that we couldn't quite work out, a sort of after taste that certainly wasn't cheese.

It took us some time to realise that the problem was excessive rennet but I've always valued the maxim that the only person who never gets it wrong is the one who does nothing.

When faced with a gallon of milk warming up in the pan, gaining in acidity from the starter, you will be tempted not to believe how tiny an amount of rennet you actually need to add. If you add half a bottle of rennet the cheese certainly will taste funny! When the recipe calls for four drops, it means four drops!

A basic soft cheese

This cheese can be prepared without a starter, but it is also good with a pot of crème fraiche added to it. It is actually an experiment to make some cheese and for the moment should be seen as nothing more than that.

You will need the following:

1 gallon (4.5 litres) of milk
*4 drops of rennet
salt
a sterile bowl to collect curds
a sterile knife
several sterile muslin sheets (cheesecloths)
a sterile stockpot
* Read the instructions to find out how your own rennet will coagulate in a gallon of milk – use too much rennet and you will end up with a product

with the density of concrete but use too little and you will have nothing more than liquid rennet.

Put the milk in the stock pot either without a starter or try a small tub of crème fraiche or some mesophilic starter. By trying it with and without you will find out how the different components can alter the flavour of your cheese. Then leave it for 30 minutes.

Add rennet – usually one drop per litre of milk. Let the label guide you! A gallon or 4.5 litres looks like a lot of milk but rennet is an enzyme and when the molecule has done its job it is simply released to do its job on the next bit of protein, so a little goes a long, long way. Rennet is dissolved in boiled, cooled water. Raise the temperature to 30⁰C.

Leave the milk, now not on the heat, to set. You will be able to feel that the surface of the milk has set like a jelly. This is almost a junket – a sweet made from milk, cream, sugar and brandy.

Looking for a clean break

It you thrust your (clean) finger into the curd it should break around it and create a small crack. In other words, you should be able to see more than just your finger in the mould, but a crack around it.

When the cheese has set you are going to cut the curds with a knife. Firstly, in a criss-cross fashion and then diagonally to make small cubes (well little rhomboid shapes really). You will notice the whey fall out of the curds and if you sprinkle a teaspoon of salt over the curds you will see even more whey come out.

Pour the curds into a colander and wash them under gently running cold water, cutting all the time. The important thing is to get as much whey out as you can.

Gather the curds into a muslin and sprinkle with 5g of salt and then combine them. You can taste the cheese to see if it is salty enough for you. You will have getting on for 400g of cheese from this so it is not going to last forever so you really do not need to over salt it. Next hang the cheesecloth on a hook and allow it to drain overnight.

Now the fun starts.

You can put the cheesecloth of what is now cottage cheese into a mould and put a heavy weight on it to make a hardish cake of

cheese or you can just smear it over fresh bread and lavish yourself with the joy of having made your first cheese. The basic cheese that you have just made is a brilliant receptacle for various other foods including:

Chives chopped up small and mixed in with the cheese, then spooned into a ramekin.
Basil finely chopped.
Garlic finely chopped. It you smear the cheese onto a piece of cling film once you have added your garlic, then coat the top surface with sesame seeds, roll the cheese, you have the ideal version of a famous French novelty cheese.
Olives spoon this cheese into the cavity of pitted olives.
Sun dried tomatoes seriously the most amazing thing you have ever tasted!

You can also use it in recipes for pasta, in fondues and on pizza. You can even add sugar and less salt and use it in sweets. You can eat it neat on crackers or with your fingers!

A basic hard cheese

This is a little more involved and often uses a thermophilic starter, the scalding of curds and certainly some pressing and ripening. It is not necessarily the pressing that makes the cheese hard, so you need to bear in mind the importance of simply following the whole recipe. And, of course, different kinds of hard cheese require different recipes to make them.

Ingredients:
1 gallon of milk
200ml of starter
4 drops of rennet (read the instructions!!)
salt
a sterile bowl to collect curds
a sterile knife
several sterile muslin sheets (cheesecloths)
a cheese mould
a cheese press or some heavy weights
a sterile stockpot

Put the milk in the stockpot with either a small tub of crème fraiche or some mesophilic starter. Leave it for 30 minutes.

Add the rennet and wait for another 30 minutes so that the curds can form. The rennet is dissolved in boiled, cooled water. The curd will probably be ready after 30 minutes – look for a clean break.

Cut the curds into 1cm squares. The curds are then scalded by increasing the temperature to around

40^{0}C, after which the curds are pitched, which means permitting them to sit at the bottom of the pan. The temperature is then increased very slowly indeed and the pitching lasts for around 30 minutes.
The whey is then ladled out and the rest is poured

into a colander lined with cheesecloth. The corners of the cheesecloth are pulled together and tied with a Stilton knot. This is done by wrapping one corner round the other three and tucking in the end. You can pull the other corners to tighten the 'bag'. This is then hung so that the rest of the whey comes out.

Steps to the Stilton Knot

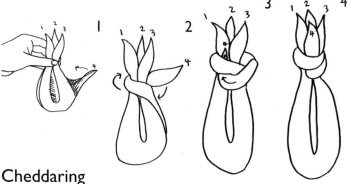

Cheddaring
When the cheesecloth is opened you will find that the curds inside will have formed a mass. These are stacked on top of each other and after 15 minutes they are rotated.

Milling
The curds are then broken by hand into small cubes of around half a centimetre and you can also add a little salt at this stage at the rate of approximately 1% by weight.

The milled curds are now placed in a mould lined with a sterile cheesecloth. The corners are folded over and the follower is put in place.

Pressing
You should begin to apply light pressure first, around 10 kilos increasing to 20 and then 40 kilos. Some presses give you an indication of the force you are exerting.

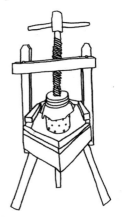

The basic idea is to increase the pressure slowly so that only whey comes out, not fat, and certainly not cheese. You might well clog the holes if you go too fiercely too quickly.

The idea is to get rid of whey and nothing els, but the process is is also intended to compact the curds enough to expel any air so that the cheese will not 'blow up' when maturing.

Drying
This is simply achieved by leaving it to dry. You might need to do this in a humidity controlled atmosphere. Some commercial cheese makers do it with fans or in special rooms. The drying process creates a rind and once this is in place the maturing stages can begin. Following drying, cheeses are matured in cool temperatures at less than 10ºC.

Bandaging and sealing

Bandaging seals the cheese and maintains its structural integrity. It is done by cutting sheets of cheesecloth to the shape, sticking them with fat and then wrapping a sterile bandage around, again sealed with fat.

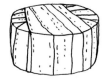

You can also seal with wax. You can buy cheese wax which is melted over a water bath and then brushed onto the rinded cheese.

Some cheeses such as Parmesan are oiled with olive oil once every three months to stop them from drying too quickly.

Maturing

The cheese is left for a number of weeks according to the recipe and during this time the flavours develop in the cheese. They are traditionally matured on wooden slatted shelves and turned upside down every couple of days.

Chapter Seven | Further Techniques

The basic cheese we made in the last chapter will open the doors for all sorts of cheese making and should whet your appetite for the whole process. There is, however, much more to cheese than just splashing a few drops of rennet around. In this chapter we are going to look at the various techniques beyond the basic manufacturing process before going on to look at making individual cheeses.

Cooking curds

Cooking curds actually contracts them a little and thus more whey comes out of the cheese. Cooking also affects the texture of the cheese and the overall nature of the final product and it reduces the amount of spoiling bacteria in the cheese, thus

allowing the bacteria you have added in your starter to grow unhindered.

Cooking the curds also makes them fuse together more easily when it comes to making a hard cheese under pressure, rather than having a lot of compressed curds actually stuck to each other as you tend to get in the crumbly basic cheese.

When you cook curds you must increase the temperature very slowly, maybe a couple of degrees every ten minutes or so. There are a couple of reasons for this. Firstly, it is difficult to control high heats and you will kill any bacteria in the cheese if the temperature gets as hot as 45–47°C. The ideal temperature is no more than 40°C and once you hit this temperature you must control the heat very carefully. The second reason is that you increase any chemical reactions going on in the cheese and if you heat it to too high a temperature you will introduce bitter flavours.

Cooking should take place for at least 30 minutes. You need a good thermometer when you are doing this, and try not to stir up the curds too much. It is not always an easy process.

You will need to know your own cooker. I find with a gallon of milk that if I keep it on a low light the temperature rises slowly. Then, when it gets to 39⁰C I turn it on full blast for just 30 seconds and then turn it off. This is enough to hold the temperature at 40⁰C for the required time.

Cheddaring

This is a process developed in Cheddar in Somerset. If it is real Cheddar cheese it is stored in Wookey Hole, a cave nearby. But you can make your own Cheddar because the name refers to the process.

After heating the curds are cut into cubes and then stacked on top of each other. They are frequently turned, which allows the whey to run out more efficiently and speeds up the maturing.

Cheddaring is also used to set the blocks of curds to the right acidity. The blocks of curds are turned over until the correct pH is obtained in the clear whey. This is usually measured by titration and is an important part of commercial cheese making. It is not all that important for home cheese making in small quantities because the act of cutting curds in a pan is sufficient.

If you have blocks of curd in either a farmhouse or a commercial facility, the number of cut cheddars will define the moisture retention of the final product. This is also regulated to some extent by the number of times the curds are turned.

You can actually buy cheddaring knives that have

parallel blades for cutting the curds and lifting them over, but these are not really necessary for small scale home production.

Acidity

Milk curdles at pH 4.6. If you add vinegar to milk it will also curdle, and if you like your cheese smelling of vinegar, this would be a good way of making it. The acidity of the cheese, after it has curdled, has an important role to play in its final make up. For this reason the acidity of the whey is often measured. A special titration rig was commonly used for maintaining consistent results. For example, we have already mentioned cheddaring until the whey reaches a certain acidity.

The skills needed for accurate titration are not all that important for the home cheese maker, especially when there are ideal alternatives. You can buy digital pH meters that give you an exact readout. They need to be buffered, that is reset to zero using distilled water. You can also buy good-old-fashioned litmus paper, although one of the suppliers now refers to them as pH papers.

Large scale commercial cheese makers will have recipes that include very fine parameters for acidity. The pH of a liquid is the inverse power of the hydrogen ion concentration. So pH7, often unhelpfully referred to as neutral, has 10^{-7}g of hydrogen ions per litre of liquid. Whey, at coagulation, has over a thousand times this amount of acidity at pH4.6 or $10^{-4.6}$g per litre.

Acidity is at its most important during the ripening process and there is no real need to be so exact for domestic cheese making, or for that matter with small scale cheese production, where a selling point can often come from the different way different batches of cheese turn out.

Pressing

When I first started making cheese I imagined that a hard cheese was created by pressing it in a mould. Well, this isn't really the whole story because you can make a hard cheese with little pressing.

We have already looked at a couple of presses and the mechanics of each of them are fairly straight forward, from a simple heavy weight on the mould to the most expensive press you can buy. It is the act of pressing that needs a little more comment.

Firstly, the reason for pressing cheese is primarily to remove whey and create a biscuit shaped piece of cheese. The full sized cheeses that you see in supermarkets and cheese shops are beyond the scope of the home producer and are created in buckets with a hydraulic press.

You can buy polythene moulds that you line with cheesecloth and into which you pour your curds. The cheesecloth is then wrapped around the top of the curds and the plunger/lid is placed on top.

There is a limit to the amount of whey you can extract by using a heavy weight so a mechanical press is much more effective.

The pressure should be gradually increased rather than blasting it in one go. First and foremost you are trying to force the liquid from within the curds, so a light pressure followed by an increasing one will do the trick. Otherwise, you will force the muslin into the holes of the press too quickly and the whole thing will block up.

Dipping

Commercial cheeses are often washed in hand hot water which causes them to become smooth. Following this they undertake a period of drying, often for a week. This period is important and the smoother the cheese surface, the better the rind that will develop. This seals in the cheese to mature.

Waxing

This is done with melted cheese wax that is bought specially for the purpose. Do not be tempted to use candle wax; it cracks and doesn't work. (Believe me, I've tried!) You melt the wax in a water bath and brush it onto the cheese. The cheese needs its own rind before you paint it. It doesn't have to be too mature, just a little. You can also dip the cheese, but don't hang around, you're not cooking it.

MAKING A BASIC CHEESE *(without rennet)*

You can use shop bought milk, either full fat or skimmed. (Full fat does give better results).

Check the temperature - this one is going to 80°C.

Add the coagulant, in this case 125ml of white vinegar.

The curds form, here not as a solid mass.

Pour the curds and whey into muslin, keeping the whey.

Drain the curds until they stop dripping.

The cheese inside the muslin bag.

Washing away the flavour of vinegar and the remains of the whey.

Place the bag into a plastic mould.

Add the follower to the top and press for a couple of hours.

Add a level teaspoon of salt.

Mix the salt into the cheese.

Refill the mould and press for 24 hours.

The pressed cheese in its muslin.

Once the techniques have been mastered you can move onto more ambitious cheeses.

A small dairy press with an assortment of cheeses.

The traditional Dutch Press.

A multi-purpose press for cheese or fruit.

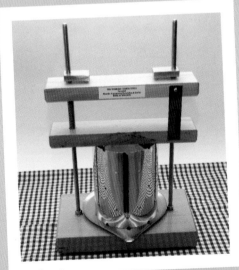

A Wheeler press worked by two screws.

Photos on this page were kindly supplied by Ascott Smallholding Supplies.

- 8 -

Moulding

Blue mould is due to the fungus Penicillium roqueforti. This is an aerobic penicillin mould that is added to the cheese at the starter stage and grows in maturing if you add air to it. You use a needle (sterile) to aerate the cheese under high humidity. I have found maturing this on a wooden board in a plastic box with a sealed lid is an ideal method. Do turn the cheese over once every few days though. You can use a skewer if you wish to bring the air into the cheese and create bands of blueness with higher acidity where the air has got in.

White mould is my personal favourite, and the probable reason for writing this book. To realise this was started over 1450 years ago is staggering, especially when you realise the number of contaminants that could have killed people over all those years. Brie and Camembert cheese is heavenly and this is due to the fungus Penicillium candidum. Again, they are best added to the cheese at the starter stage but some preparations do call for spraying it over the surface. I personally am not keen on sprays because I worry about all that fungus getting into my lungs (yes I know it's supposed to be all right).

Also, if you do it unevenly then you get too much mould on one side and not enough on the other. It does do heavenly things to the cheese though!

Both penicillium moulds need a temperature of around 10°C to start off but should be a little cooler when they are maturing. You will find all the specific instructions on the packet.

One big problem is using a sachet that is designed for 50 litres or more of milk for a single gallon. You do need a reliable set of scales. Remember also that a gallon is 4.54 litres, so don't get confused.

Chapter Eight | When it All Goes Wrong

In our home we started making basic cheese some years ago with milk bought from the supermarket. We didn't believe that such a small amount of rennet would solidify such a huge volume of milk, so we added more, and more, and more. Consequently, the cheese tasted funny. But we ate it and thought it was beautiful until someone piped up, "This tastes funny!" And it did too.

There are all sorts of reasons for cheese tasting funny but it is not always as a result of you having done something wrong.

When the cheese tastes funny

This might be due to circumstances as above, but it could also be due to bad hygiene or not sterilising equipment and so on. This is really important because in making cheese you are actually growing whatever bugs were on the utensils, in the pans, on your hands and in the milk. Just looking clean is never enough; all your utensils have to be sterile.

It is such an important issue that might be brought into focus by the fact that it would be illegal to make cheese in the school laboratory because you simply do not know what microbes you are growing. The moral: sterilise!

When your cheese tastes sharp

This is an acidity problem and is caused when you have added too much starter, or left it too long before you added rennet. It can also occur if the rennet is not removed from the curds properly. The acidity of a moist cheese will increase as the bacteria continue to produce acid until eventually the increase kills the bacteria.

No curds

This occurs if the milk is too cold or there is not enough rennet or it is out of date. It could occur if the milk contains a lot of antibiotics and the bacteria have been killed off before they have done their work.

If you have used Milton or something similar to sterilise your equipment and left some of it in the bottom of the pan you might have accidentally sterilised your starter; it happened to me once.

Fizzy or alcoholic cheese

Sometimes you can introduce yeast into your milk and this starts to ferment the sugars into alcohol. There is a drink called Kefir that is supposed to be good for you but I'll stick to Mild thanks. The home cheese maker is likely to experience this if they have been making bread or brewing beer, and it is another reason for having a separate dairy.

A fizzy cheese might end up having holes in it because the fermentation process will give off CO_2 gas.

Hard cheese

Rubber consistencies occur when the cheese is overheated, or is not ripened enough or has been made with too much rennet. The flavour of unripened cheese is not good either and is usually bland. But here I have to digress. Any cheese you make yourself tastes wonderful!

Wet or dry

This is a function of the size of the curds. Smaller curds, when cut, can lose too much water or larger curds too little. So your cheese will be either too wet or too dry. A wet cheese is likely to be too sharp as the whey inside will have increased in acidity.

Don't forget: whey is the bit that goes off! A wet cheese will certainly have a tendency to go off.

Storing cheese

Most people put cheese in the fridge, which is a dreadful thing to do if you are fussy about how the cheese actually tastes. This leads us to the inevitable conclusion that modern kitchens are too small and the only place you have left to store food is the fridge.

A number of animals and pests are after your cheeses, from the ordinary house fly, who will lay her eggs on it, to the domestic cat who will kill for a sly nibble. So make sure wherever you store your cheese that it is completely animal proof. Any commercial cheesemaking should also have an electric fly killer installed.

The maturation of domestic cheese can take place in a cool area that is not too high in humidity, which will encourage maturity without fungal infections.

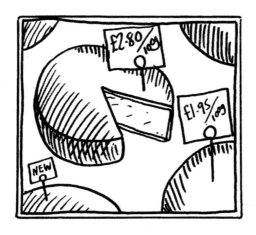

Chapter Nine | Thinking of Selling?

People who have read my other books will realise by now that the major thrust of writing them is to encourage people to make their own food and to be responsible for their own provisions. Who knows? One day we might all need to rely on these skills!

There is a great movement today to sell up and go and buy some acres of land and pay for it by either getting yet another job, or making a few bob by selling produce from those few acres.

One lady I know spends all her days filling boxes with vegetables she has grown on the smallholding and selling them to her forty odd customers. She has a hard job to make ends meet and she works all the time. She cannot compete with supermarkets.

If she could then the supermarkets would not think twice about lowering their prices until they won, even if it meant they would lose out on a particular product.

Economics

As I write this I am making a cheese. Home reared, the milk would have cost me around 50 pence. Tomorrow I will have some cheese that could be sold for around £3.00. In my local supermarket the same product will be on sale for around the same price. But this is my food. I can enhance this basic cottage cheese with all kinds of flavours and consequently can up the cost a bit. But I have to be sure that I can get my cheese to market. So sort your market first, then your product.

Regulations

In recent years the rules affecting food production and sale have been unified across Europe and in the UK there is a very strict regime that everyone must follow, regardless of the size of the company. Everyone has to go through this process regardless of the number of employees. Talk to your local food authority and they will help. Certainly it is easier for a one man band than a big company, but not all that much – you still have to prove you can produce a safe product.

As the first step on the road to manufacture and sales you should make contact with your Local

Area Food Inspector to explain your plans and they will send you all the relevant booklets that you need to plan your business. The Town Hall will have the contact details. But do remember that if you register too soon you might not be ready for the Inspector to look at your premises.

You should ideally register your intention to produce food for the public with your Local Area Food Inspector no later than a month before you plan to start producing in order to give the Food Inspector a chance to visit you and to talk you through what he is looking for and to assess the appropriateness of your facilities.

You will have to register if you only produce one or two products a week or if you produce hundreds of tonnes of cheese and you will need a documented food safety system. This will not simply be a paperwork exercise but something you can prove you actually do to guarantee, at each stage of the production, storage, transport and sales process, that you have in place all the appropriate safegaurds to protect the health of your prospective customers.

You will also need to document the processes by which you prove and adhere to cleanliness and contamination control. How will you separate the different inputs into the business, be they raw meat, milk or vegetables, and guarantee they are fit for consumption? How will you prove the age and suitability of your raw materials and how will you know if something has gone wrong?

You will need to prove that you can recognise when something has gone wrong at each stage of the process and, perhaps more importantly, how you will react to put things right.

The basic rules might be different from locality to locality because they are designed to reflect the region in which the food is produced, but the same high standards are fundamental to all areas so the best advice if you are thinking of making and selling farmhouse food is to make contact with your food inspector at the Local Authority, and they will talk you through the processes and help you to plan your business.

Milk

If you produce your own milk, your animal(s) will have to be tested and the milk will need to be tested too. This will be a major part of the cost to your business. Otherwise, you will have to prove the safety of your milk and how you handle it from the point of purchase to its final disposal. Should you wish to produce your cheese using un-pasteurised milk then expect further hurdles to negotiate in demonstrating its safety to the appropriate authorities.

Labelling

You cannot call your cheese Brie or Camembert

unless you make it there. The locals tend to get upset because they have protected the name, even though you may make Brie better than they do. You could choose to call it 'Brie type cheese that was made at 47 Honeywell Lane' and it would probably be a safe bet that no one else would want to copy your unique product description!

Legally you have to be very careful if you are going to call a cheese something which people will recognise as a familiar product. It probably would not be a problem until you start making a lot of money but then they will all want a bit.

Gourmet

There are hundreds of cheese clubs around the country. You could make a living by contacting these to demonstrate precisely how your cheese is made, then sell the cheese based on its uniqueness or its exceptional quality. You will find many cheese clubs associated with universities. The University College London Cheese Club states that they are 'guaranteed cheaper than death and funnier than heroin.' So you might be in for some fun!

There are a number of other, more formal, cheese societies, many associated with the county standards. Each year the County Agricultural Societies run their own competitions and they are the custodians of the standards for their particular cheeses.

Shows

Frome and Nantwich both hold annual cheese shows and there are many others that do the same. You will find lots of producers and individuals who are in a similar position to yourself, and it is well worth going to visit them. There is great competition and secrecy about small producer cheeses, but when it comes to helpfulness you will look far to find a better set of people.

Chapter Ten | Showing Off

At one time there were cheese shows in every village and district in the country. People would show their cheeses or cheese products and cheese making clubs and associations were commonplace. Individual farmers produced the cheeses that were sold in the shops and on market stalls and it was a great marketing advantage to be able to sell their prize winning cheese along with their eggs and butter.

On market stalls today you can still find locally made cheese and dairy products but they are few and far between. The local cheese wire, the news for cheese makers, stopped printing and in the end the cheese world has lost out. Local shows are still full of 'seven beans on a plate' produce classes, but it is the aim of this book to encourage people back into showing their home made cheeses again.

In Britain we still have the world's biggest cheese shows at Nantwich and Frome. In each show there are a number of classes, some for professional cheese makers, some for others. Nearly all the county shows still have a cheese section with classes open for non professional entries. Of course, if you are thinking of making your own cheese for sale then you should put them up in the show for a number of good reasons. Firstly, it is good to be able to say that yours is a prize winning cheese. Secondly, it is easier to get the bank to provide some cash if you can make a product so good that it has beaten everyone else in the county. Finally, it encourages you to hone your skills and you pick up so many ideas and tips.

What is the point of doing anything badly? Competitions are not to see how good one person is, i.e. the winner, but are about improving the overall standards. I suppose this is a bit of a plea to everyone reading this book to get out there and either organise or take part in cheese making competitions. This goes particularly for the smallholding societies.

Shows are usually split into sections, each of which has a schedule for the various competitions. There might be as many as fifty shedules, i.e. fifty different competitions going on at any one time. These might be single Farmhouse, traditional Cheshire, white any weight, white over 2kg, traditional Cheddar or coloured Cheddar and so on. Before the entry schedule there will be overall schedules that have to be adhered to, for example:

'All cheeses are to be cylindrically pressed, bandaged, or waxed and presented on a single board or a white plate.'

If your cheese is bandaged and wrapped in cling film, and you forget to unwrap the cling film, you will not progress very far. Other ideas about display, like putting some fruit around the cheese, will similarly disqualify it should this be contrary to the schedule.

Marks identifying the cheese, except for those given by the society, are not allowed and advertising material is usually only allowed after the judging has taken place. Excessive ironing and boring of cheeses is also not allowed, probably because it reflects on the processes by which a cheese has been made in the first place.

The exhibitors dress should reflect the dairy and no one but the judges are allowed around the cheeses from a specified time until after the judging has taken place. In certain circumstances this will involve security.

The schedule for each part of the show has to be adhered to exactly and the judges are looking to score the cheeses against the schedule requirements and nothing else. If you keep to the description for the particular class you are competing in you will win a prize. Only when the differentiation between the very best and minor placings are worked out does it become fiercely competitive. So it is possible, for example, to be a novice cheese maker and gain a 'Highly Recommended' rosette and as there are also classes for novice cheese makers too you might be able to enter both classes of competition with the same cheese.

What makes a good cheese?

It goes without saying that the cheese has to taste right. But there is much more to it than that. For a start, the cheeses that are in this book would not do for a national competition because there simply isn't enough cheese in a gallon of milk to make a competition cheese. You will have to progress to larger equipment. This is not the case for local shows, however.

The water contents of cheeses are very strictly controlled in some classes and this will have to be taken into account. The rind quality, should it be wrapped and for how long it is matured are all a factor. If you are planning to show your cheeses then you will have to plan when the cheese is actually started in order for it to peak on the day of the show.

Chapter Eleven | Notes on the Recipes

For the most part, these recipes are for a single gallon of milk and can be easily produced in the kitchen. A gallon is used simply because this is the size of a large domestic stockpot and is probably the most convenient starting point for domestic cheese making. A gallon of milk is also just about as much as you can conveniently handle in the average kitchen. Of course, you can add more if you wish, doubling the numbers or even tripling them.

As with all our food books, the recipes are a pretty accurate guide, but are to be experimented with in order to make your own unique products. You will find, however, that there is less scope for experimentation with cheese making than, say, making sausages.

The idea behind this book, and indeed all the series of books including *The Smoking and Curing Book, The Sausage Book,* and any that might follow, is that people can do these recipes at home for themselves. You may not have a smallholding but you will have a kitchen. Maybe these books will inspire you to get your own place in the country at some time in the future.

Another point to remember is that cheese has been made for millennia, and any ideas you might have will probably already have been considered. But not necessarily! We have lost considerable knowledge in these modern times although we sometimes give the impression we believe we know everything. So get your pencil out and scribble all over the book with amendments and changes. If you have a mind to try ancient cheeses such as *Queso blanco* or *Mrs Mehra's Paneer* recipe, then there are some recipes for you as well as some very specialised ones.

If you are new to cheese making then have a go at the basic recipe found earlier in the book and experiment away with this. Soon you will want to move on to new and more challenging cheeses. There are hours of fun to be had buying cheeses and then coming back to try and make them yourself. A gallon of milk will yield approximately a pound of cheese, and at current prices you will be making high quality cheese at cheap cheese prices, so don't make cheese only to compete on price!

We have excluded a number of cheeses because they are best made in larger quantities, and trying to make, say, a Dunlop Cheese, which is not that much removed from what we used to call a 'cooking' cheese, seems to be a little out of the scope of what we are trying to do here. As an example, if you are going to produce a cheddar and plan to do so in greater volumes it is possible to halt the first batch at the cheddaring point and combine this with cut curds from the next batch, thus giving you a bigger quantity to go at.

There is even a recipe for cheating cheese. This is where you combine your basic curds as detailed earlier and mix them with a blended cheese that you have bought from the shops. Blue cheese is a good one for this. Your own curds will be mixed with a small amount of your favourite blue and then off you go. Do be careful to avoid contamination from the packaging if you do this, but it is really good fun.

For accuracy and to avoid any confusion we have referred to the amount of milk required as 4.5 litres. This means a gallon, but it will not really matter too much if you use two 2 litre bottles from the supermarket.

All the recipes are for pasteurised milk. If you want to use un-pasteurised it's up to you. We have already discussed the basic reasons for pasteurising and how to do it. You can easily add this process to each recipe.

Commercial cheese producers

To be honest this book will only whet the appetite for anyone contemplating selling his or her own cheeses. There is lots of help out there to be found in the resources section. You will, however, be able gain an idea about which type of cheese is best for you, whether it is Cheddar or a garlic roule. On the whole, the basic recipe is based on 4% starter and 25ml of rennet per 100 litres of milk.

Using a starter

If a recipe calls for a starter it will say something like 'add 200ml of mesophilic starter' which means 200ml of cultured liquid you have produced either from your own recipe or have made up separately. The list of starters and other materials can be found in the resources section and, as you will now be aware, you can use starters already cultured in milk or simply inoculate the cheese batch with a pinch or two from the starter packet.

Using rennet

Don't just drop the rennet into the milk; it might well start working in lumps. Instead, add your rennet to a quarter of a cup of very lukewarm water and use this. Some bright spark in our house who will remain nameless added rennet to a tablespoon of milk. It set hard and ended up being thrown around the kitchen!

Using calcium chloride

When you pasteurise milk, and most shop bought milk is pasteurised, the amount of calcium ions in the milk is reduced. This is important in that it helps the coagulation process. You can replace this calcium by adding calcium chloride. For a single gallon of milk you only need a gram, so dissolve a level teaspoon of it in a cup of water. Pour half of this away and then use only half of what remains.

This way you will get a firmer curd that will not fall apart when you stir it. The recipes will not state anything about Calcium chloride unless it is completely necessary. The best thing to do is to experiment to see if you feel you need to use it. I personally have never found it necessary but perhaps my milk supply is different from yours, so give it a try and see what you think.

It was John Seymour who said that real culture was whatever we did to make life bearable. Applying this test, cheese making is really cultured!

Aberffraw Cheese

As I am writing this in Wales I thought I would include the ancient Welsh cheesemaking that probably was much the same all over the country. Abberfraw was the capital of the ancient Kings of Gwynedd, where tales of Gelert the wolfhound and de-bearding horses abound (but that's another book!)

Ingredients:

4.5 litres of really creamy milk
I pot of buttermilk as a starter
Some Ladies bedstraw liquor *(Ladies Bedstraw is a plant that was used as a coagulant. Boil up a good handful of Ladies Bedstraw in a litre of water for 15 minutes, simmer gently until it has reduced by half. Strain and then add a teaspoon to a cup of milk and see how it works. From the results you should then gauge how much you need).*

Instructions:

Mix the milk and cream and heat them to 28°C.
Add the cultures and wait for 90 minutes at a constant temperature.
Add the bedstraw liquor and allow an hour for the curds to form. (It could be straight away or it might take longer – experiment!)

Cut the curds to 1cm cubes.
Pour them into a cheesecloth lined colander and drain for 20 minutes.
Wash with cooled, boiled water then draw up the corners and squeeze-drain the cheese.
Spoon out the cheese when the dripping stops, then add either some milk, cream, honey or salt depending what you want to do with it.

Basic Goat Cheese

Goat cheese tends not to be pressed and is always handled carefully. It taints easily so be careful not to use rubber gloves and make sure there are no aromas around the preparation area. This cheese does not require rennet but you can use it if you wish.

Ingredients:

4.5 litres of fresh goat's milk, which might be more than one day's milking.
The juice of four lemons or 50ml of white vinegar or 4 drops of rennet in a little cooled, boiled water.
Cheese cloth.

Instructions

Heat the milk to 80°C and add the acid, stirring to mix.
Leave them for 30 minutes, allowing the mix to cool to 40°C.
Cut the curd into 1cm cubes and gently pour them into a cheesecloth lined colander.
Draw the corners and hang to drain the whey.

Some writers say you can vary the cheese type in the hanging process. An hour and it is similar to ricotta. Three hours and it becomes like cream cheese and six hours it becomes quite hard and can be pushed into a mould to be lightly pressed.

You can sweeten the cheese - honey is best. Salt it to 1% by weight if you wish to keep it longer than a week or so.

Blue Stilton Cheese

The creaminess of this cheese is legendary, so much so that it is called the King of Cheeses, by the English anyway!

Ingredients:

4.5 litres of milk.
100ml of mesophilic starter solution.
4 drops of rennet in a little cooled, boiled water.
1g (an eighth of a teaspoon) of Penicillium roqueforti.
Salt.

Instructions:

Add the starter to the milk and warm them slowly until they reache 30°C.
Add the rennet and stir well. Leave them for 30 minutes.
When the curd forms. ladle it into a cheesecloth and tie it up for an hour, tightening the bag as time progresses to remove the whey.
Sprinkle it with 10g of salt and add the Penicillium roqueforti, previously added to a little salted water.

There are various ways to progress. You can either pack it into lined moulds and press it lightly for two hours or you can pack it into unlined moulds without pressing.

Either way, you will need a cheese that will turn easily in the mould. Turn the cheese over in the mould every day for a week. Rub a little vegetable oil into the surface and leave it for another week in a container at around 10°C with a bowl of water near it to increase the humidity.

After the week, remove it and pierce it all over with a sterile needle. Two weeks later, the mould will have formed.

Boursin Cheese

These cheeses are made in different ways. Ours is a cottage cheese with various additives determining the flavours. Traditionally it is flavoured with horseradish and garlic.

Ingredients:

4.5 litres of milk.
100ml of mesophilic starter solution (buttermilk is good).
4 drops of rennet in a little cooled, boiled water.
Salt.
5g of grated horseradish.
1 clove of grated garlic.

Instructions:

Heat the milk to 20°C and add the 100ml of mesophilic culture.
Leave it for 30 minutes.
Add 2-3 drops of liquid rennet and stir it in well.
Cover the pot and allow the milk to set at room temperature for at least 12 hours, when curds of the right flavour will form.
Plop the whole curd into a muslin bag or a cheesecloth with the corners pulled together.
Hang it up to dry for at least 8 hours.
Mix in 1% by weight of salt.

Mix in the horseradish and garlic and beat the whole well with a fork to make a homogenous mixture. The cheese is then packed into ramekins and kept refrigerated.

To serve, heat the outside of the ramekin in boiling water and tip the contents out to be wrapped in vine leaves. A fantastic buffet presentation!

Brie

This was probably the first cheese to be used as a tax. It is amazing to think it was first made some 1600 years ago.

Ingredients:

4.5 of litres milk.
50ml of mesophilic starter solution.
1g (one eighth of a teaspoon) of Penicillium candidum
3 drops of rennet in a small amount of cooled, boiled water.

Instructions:

Add the starter and the culture of Penicillium candidum to the milk and slowly warm them to 32°C.
Leave them for 30 minutes at this temperature.
Add the rennet and leave it for up to four hours for the curd to form. (Lower the rennet quantity, and the curds will form more slowly).
Carefully, but throughly, cut the curd into 0.5cm cubes.
Drain off most of the whey and ladle the curds into moulds so that they are no deeper than 8 cm.
Leave the curds to drain overnight and then carefully turn them out of the moulds and onto a cheese mat. Sprinkle salt over the sides and top and, when you have turned the cheese over, sprinkle salt on the top.
Over the next couple of days, turn the cheeses over and over every 8 hours or so, salting as you go, but only using pinches of salt. If kept in fairly humid conditions they will start to become mouldy on the outside. At this point you can simply leave the cheese to ripen.
The characteristic white mould is working the cheese inside.
After a week it will be quite mature and after five weeks it will be like soup! You will need to check the cheese daily and should eat it when it is just right for you!

Caerphilly

It is called Caerphilly because you have to do it carefully.

Ingredients:

4.5 litres of milk.
100ml of mesophilic starter.
4 drops of rennet in a little cooled, boiled water.
Salt.

Instructions:

Warm the milk to 20°C.
Add the starter and heat them to 34°C and add the rennet.
Stir well and leave for 30 minutes.
When the curd forms, cut it into 1cm cubes and gently stir
it for 15 minutes.
Allow the curd to settle for 15 minutes.
Raise the temperature slowly over an hour to 34°C, stirring
the whole time.
Salt to 1% by weight and pack the warm curds into a mould
lined with a moist cheesecloth.
Apply light pressure overnight, then float the cheese in a
brine made from 300g of salt in a litre of water. (You might
need more than a litre). The cheese should float.
After 24 hours, place the cheese to dry and it should be
ready in a month.

Camembert

This recipe calls for the curds to be sprayed with Penicillium candidum culture at the ripening stage. To do this you will need one of those household sprayers. Sterilise it with a hypochlorite solution by filling it and carefully spraying the contents through the nozzle. Then spray cooled, boiled water through and rinse the outside the same as the inside. To make the culture spray, dilute 2g of Penicillium candidum in a litre of water with half a teaspoon of salt.

Ingredients:

4.5 litres of good quality pasteurised milk.
50ml of mesophilic starter solution.
1g (one eighth of a teaspoon) of Penicillium candidum.
4 drops of rennet in a small amount of cooled, boiled water.

Instructions:

Add the starter to the milk and slowly warm it to 30°C.
Leave it for 30 minutes at this temperature.
Add the rennet and leave it for an hour for the curd to form. Then ladle the curd directly into moulds no deeper than 10cm.
Leave the curds to drain overnight and then carefully turn them out of the moulds and onto a cheese mat. Sprinkle salt over the sides and top and, when you have turned the cheese over, sprinkle salt on the top.
Spray the cheeses with Penicillium candidum and, over the next couple of days, turn the cheeses over and over every 8 hours or so, salting as you go, by rubbing in pinches of salt. Stop salting after two days and then, ten or so days later, the cheeses should be ready. You will need to check the cheese daily after a fortnight and, as with Brie, you should eat it when it is just right for you!

Cheating Blue Cheese

This is a basic cheese with an inoculation at the cheese moulding stage.

Ingredients:

4.5 litres of fresh milk.
100ml of mesophilic starter culture.
8 drops of rennet in a small quantity of cooled, boiled water.
1 tablespoon of mashed blue cheese.
Cheese cloth.

Instructions:

Combine the milk with the starter and leave them for an hour at room temperature.
Add the rennet to the milk.
Cover and set them aside to set overnight at 20°C.
Ladle the curds into a colander lined with fine cheesecloth.
Drain for around 8 hours, then draw up the corners of the cloth and hang until the whey is removed.
Add the mashed up blue cheese and 1% salt by weight and mix them well.
Place them into a mould and press, under medium weight, for 2 hours.
Remove from the mould and store in a sterile, lidded plastic container for a couple of weeks.
Pierce the cheese all over with a sterile knitting needle.
In a month the blue will have formed and the cheese will be edible, but better if ripened for another month.

Be careful with your inoculation cheese. It must be kept in sterile conditions and scrupulously germ free. You can inport all sorts of nasties if you are not careful.

Cheddar

Cheddar originally came from Somerset and is made using a process that has become known as cheddaring. This involves collecting the curd and stacking it, one on top of another, and then rotating the order of stacking.

Ingredients:

4.5 litres of fresh milk.
100ml of mesophilic starter culture.
6 drops of rennet in a little cooled, boiled water.
5g of salt.

Instructions:

Warm the milk to 32°C and add the starter, mixing well.
Leave for 1 hour at this temperature.
Add the rennet and stir constantly with a whisk for 5 minutes.
Allow the cheese to set for 2 hours and then cut the curds into 0.5cm cubes.
Leave the curds to sit for 15 minutes.
Over an hour, raise the temperature to 39°C, gently stirring to keep the curds separate.
Leave at this temperature for another hour.
Drain the curds into a colander lined with a cheesecloth.
Cut the combined curds into three pieces and stack them, one on top of another. This is cheddaring. Rotate the order of the cheeses every 15 minutes.
After 45 miutes, transfer the curds to a cheesecloth lined mould and press lightly for an hour.
Flip the cheese over and press moderatly for three hours.
Flip the cheese and then press hard for 24 hours.
Leave the cheese to ripen in the fridge, uncovered at first for a week, then under a dish for 3 months.

Cheshire Cheese

My own favourite and the perfect mate to a pickled onion!

Ingredients:

4.5 litres of milk.
100ml of mesophilic starter solution (buttermilk is good).
4 drops of rennet in a little cooled, boiled water.
Salt.

Instructions:

Add the starter to the milk and slowly warm it to 29°C and leave for 30 minutes.
Add the rennet and leave for another 30 minutes to form the curd.
Cut the curds into 1cm cubes and increase the temperature to 35°C over about 30 minutes, then allow the curds to settle for 30 minutes.
Ladle the whey out from the pan and cut the curds into 10 cm squares and pile them at the back of the vessel. Draw off all the whey and allow the curds to drain in this position. Move the position of the blocks every 30 minutes for 90 minutes.
Once drained, break up the curds into 1cm pieces and add 1% by weight of salt.
Place it into a mould lined with cheesecloth and press lightly overnight.
The following day, increase it to full pressure and keep this up for 2 more days, opening and turning the cheese.
Put it in storage, turning it every couple of days. The cheese will be ready in 3 weeks.

You can lard this cheese but I have never done this.

Chevre Cheese

Some recipes use suitably rustic alternatives to whey. Fill a stockpot with nettles, add a litre of water, bring it to the boil with the lid on and simmer it for an hour to wilt the nettles, then boil it until the liquor has reduced by half. 100ml of this will quite capably turn the milk.

This is a really simple cheese and is little more than the coagulated curds simply drained in a muslin.

Ingredients:

4.5 of litres milk.
100ml of nettle juice or 4 drops of rennet in a little cooled, boiled water.

Instructions:

Heat the milk to 30°C.
Add the coagulant and wait for 30 minutes.
Drain it into a cheesecloth lined colander and hang it for six hours. Then squeeze it into a ball shape and run off the excess whey. Store it in a cheesecloth in the fridge.

This cheese is often stored in leaves or rolled in seeds, finely chopped chives or finely chopped mint.

Colby Cheese

This is a milder, and quicker Cheddar type of cheese. It is made in much the same way but is more tolerant of temperature and times. It is not matured as long either. Some people add colouring to the cheese, but this recipe doesn't call for it.

Ingredients:

4.5 litres of milk.
400ml of buttermilk.
6 drops of rennet in a little cooled, boiled water.
Salt to taste.

Instructions:

Add the buttermilk to the milk and warm them slowly until they reaches 29°C.
Add the rennet and stir well, then leave for 30 minutes.
When the curd forms, cut it into 1 cm cubes and gently stir them for 15 minutes.
Slowly raise the temperature to 38°C and keep at this temperature for 30 minutes, stirring from time to time.
Pour into a cheesecloth lined colander and allow the whey to drain. Add salt to 1% by weight then mix carefully.
Continue to drain for 20 minutes.
Press for 12 hours, slowly increasing the pressure until it becomes heavy.
Dry the cheese for a week in the fridge and then eat it.

You can wax it if you want to keep it for longer than a couple of weeks.

Colwick Cheese

The village of Colwick in Nottinghamshire was one of the haunts of Robin Hood, so we are told. Among its further claims to fame is this cheese which was made everywhere in the country by poor people.

Today we think that off milk is bad, but actually, it is only acidic. If you let a pint of milk go off, then the acidity will increase until the curds form. Pour this into a muslin bag and it will drain.

Ingredients:

Milk, as much as you want!

Instructions:

Keep the milk at room temperature for a week. Milk straight from the cow will take only a couple of days.
Pour the curds into a muslin bag and allow them to drain.
If you do not like the smell, then wash the curds in gently running water.
If you like soft cheese then use it as it comes out of the bag, otherwise give it a squeeze to make a harder cheese.
You can salt the cheese to 1% by weight to make a savoury cheese or you can add a tablespoon of sugar for a sweet cheese.

Traditionally Colwick cheese was served with a dished centre into which was placed all kinds of flavouring; strawberries and other soft fruit, apples, pears etc. Or it could contain onion, garlic (or ransomes, originally) or pieces of bread. It was also combined with cream in the hollowed out dish and people would spoon the two together.

Cottage Cheese

This is just like our basic cheese in the earlier part of the book and is easy to make. It is also known as farmer's cheese and smallholder's cheese.

Ingredients:

4.5 litres of fresh milk.
100ml of mesophilic starter culture.
4 drops of rennet.
Cheese cloth.

Instructions:

Combine the milk with the starter.
Leave for it for 30 minutes at room temperature and then add the rennet in a small quantity of cooled, boiled water.
Cover and set aside to set overnight at 20°C.
Cut the curd into 1 cm cubes.
Allow the curds to firm up for 15 minutes.
Increase the temperature to 43°C and cook it at this temperature for 45 minutes, but do not allow the curds to burn.
The curds are cooked when they have shrunk and fallen in the whey.
Line a colander with the cheesecloth and drain the curds for 15 minutes.
Plunge the curds into iced water for 5 minutes.
Drain the curds and place them in a bowl.
Season with a teaspoon of salt. You can add herbs, if you wish.

You can also add cream, if you wish.

Cream Cheese #1

Make this from full fat milk - a bucketful of Jersey would be wonderful. You can also mix a pint of cream with the gallon of milk (Oops! That's 450ml cream with 4.5 litres of milk).
of

Ingredients:

4.5 litres of milk (the creamier the better).
100ml of mesophilic culture.
4 drops of liquid rennet.

Instructions:

Warm the milk to 20°C and add 200ml of mesophilic culture.
Leave it for 30 minutes.
Add 2-3 drops of liquid rennet and stir it well.
Cover the pot and allow the milk to set at room temperature for at least 12 hours, when curds of the right flavour will form.
Plop the whole curd into a muslin bag or a cheesecloth with the corners pulled together.
Hang to dry for at least 8 hours.
Mix in 1% by weight of salt.
Collect herbs, fruit and anything you would like to increase the flavour.
Spoon it into a container and store it in the fridge, where it will keep for up to 2 weeks.

Cream Cheese #2

This is creamier than the previous recipe and calls for equal quantities of milk and cream. You can only eat it as part of a strict training regime incorporating a five mile run both before and after the meal.

Ingredients:

1 litre of whole milk.
1 litre of double cream.
100ml of mesophilic starter solution.
2 drops of rennet in some cooled, boiled water.

Instructions:

Carefully mix the cream and milk and warm them to 26°C.
Add your rennet and leave in a warm place overnight to curdle. It should look like yoghurt.
Drain into a cheesecloth (2 layers at least) lined colander.
Tie up the corners and drain for at least 12 hours, or until the drips have completely stopped.
Transfer it to the fridge in a sealed container where it should last for up to 5 days.

You can add all kinds of additional flavours.

Creamy Lancashire Cheese

Someone said that Lancashire was all right but better when flavoured with sage or parsley. Great God! Don't go saying that round Bacup or Rochdale way and certainly not in Longridge near Preston, where some of the best Creamy Lancashire cheeses are made.

Ingredients:

4.5 litres of milk.
400ml of buttermilk as a starter.
400ml of cream.
6 drops of rennet in a little cooled, boiled water.
Salt.

Instructions:

Add the buttermilk and the cream to the milk and warm them slowly until they reach 30°C.
Add the rennet and stir well,then leave for 30 minutes.
When the curd forms, cut it into 1cm cubes and gently stir it for 15 minutes.
Allow the curd to settle for 30 minutes.
Pour it into a cheesecloth lined colander and allow the whey to drain. Add salt to 1% by weight and mix carefully.
Continue to drain for 30 minutes, then place the cheese into lined moulds.
Press for 48 hours, slowly increasing the pressure until it becomes heavy.

You can wax or bandage the cheese and it should be completely wonderful in a month.

Danish Blue

All blue cheeses take a little work and require a bit more experience. Start early in the morning!

Ingredients:

4.5 litres of really creamy milk.
100ml of mesophilic starter culture.
1g (an eighth of a teaspoon) of Penicillium roqueforti.
6 drops of rennet in a little cooled, boiled water.
Salt.

Instructions:

Mix the milk and starter and heat them to 34°C.
Keep them at this temperature for 15 minutes.
Add the Penicillium roqueforti and wait for another hour, keeping them at a constant temperature.
Add the rennet and stir in well with a whisk.
After an hour, when set, cut the curds into 4 cm cubes and allow to rest for another hour at the same temperature.
Pour off the whey and carefully transfer the curds into a cheesecloth lined colander and drain for 20 minutes.
Sprinkle with 5g of salt.
Spoon the curds into a mould and put the lid of a saucer on the top. Turn the cheese every 30 minutes for four hours.
Remove the cheese and rub salt into all the surfaces and store it in the fridge for 3 days.
Pierce the cheese all over with a sterile needle and then keep it at around 5°C at high humidity. I use a lidded plastic box with a little bowl of water inside.
Ten days later it should be blueing nicely but it can take a couple of months. Use a sterile knife to remove any mould from the surface and remove the lid daily for 20 days to let the air circulate around the cheese.

Derby Cheese

Derby is a mild cheese with quite a high fat content. It is slightly flakier than Cheddar and not as crumbly as Cheshire. Sage Derby is a marbled version that is dyed by using powdered sage or spinach.

Ingredients:

4.5 litres of fresh milk.
100ml of mesophilic starter culture.
4 drops of rennet in a little cooled, boiled water.
Salt.

Instructions:

Warm the milk to 22°C and add the starter, mixing well.
Leave for 1 hour while you raise the temperature to 30°C.
Add the rennet and stir in, then leave it for 40 minutes for the curd to form.
Cut the curds into 2cm cubes and leave for 10 minutes.
Over an hour raise the temperature to 35°C, gently stirring to keep the curds separate.
Leave it at this temperature for 20 minutes.
Ladle the curds out and cut it into 3 blocks, which you pile on top of each other. For the next two hours reorder the pile, or if the curds cannot be separated, re-cut and pile again, every 20 minutes.
Break up the curds into 1cm cubes and add salt at 1% by weight.
Transfer the curds to a cheesecloth lined mould and press them lightly for 6 hours.
The next day, transfer them into a dry cheesecloth and mould and press lightly for a further 6 hours.
Lard and bandage the cheese and leave it to store for 2 months, turning it daily.

Edam Cheese

This is the archetypal Dutch cheese that is usually waxed. They are sometimes coloured with cheese-dye but I don't bother myself. The texture comes from the starter and scalding of the cheese and not the pressing, which is light

Ingredients:

4.5 litres of fresh milk.
100ml of thermophilic starter culture.
4 drops of rennet.
Cheese cloth.

Instructions:

Combine the milk with the starter.
Increase the temperature slowly to 32°C.
Leave it for 30 minutes at room temperature and add the rennet in a small quantity of cool, boiled water.
Leave it for 30 minutes and then cut the curds into 1cm cubes.
Increase the temperature to 38°C while gently stirring.
Allow the curds to settle for 40 minutes and then carefully pour off the whey.
Wash the curds in boiled water that has been allowed to cool to being a little cooler than hand warm.
Line a colander with a cheesecloth and drain the curds for 15 minutes, then add 1% by weight of salt.
Press the cheese for a day on either side with light pressure.
Authentically, the cheese is brined at this point (though I have enjoyed it as it is, a dreadful thing to do, I know).
Brine the cheese in a weak solution (200g per litre) for two days, turning the cheese over every few hours.
Leave it to dry and then wax it. Red is the traditional colour.
Then allowit to stand for a month.

Feta cheese

This comes from all over the countries of South Eastern Europe such as Greece, Bulgaria, and Albania. Each of them have little variation in how the cheese is made, some using specific starters, others simply using buttermilk. This recipe actually comes from Bulgaria and uses buttermilk as a starter.

Ingredients:

4.5 litres of milk.
450ml buttermilk.
8 drops of rennet.

Instructions:

Heat the milk to 32°C and then add the buttermilk.
Leave it for an hour, stirring from time to time.
Add rennet and stir it in, leaving it for 40 minutes to set.
Cut it into 1cm cubes and leave it in the whey for 20 minutes.
Ladle the curds and whey into Feta moulds or colander.
Leave them overnight to drain.
The cheese will shrivel and combine.
Take the block out of the mould and cutit into 3 to 4 pieces..
Salt all sides of the pieces.
Leave it at room temperature for 24 hours, turning the cheese pieces at least 5 or 6 time during that period.
Re-salt the wet areas where the whey has been drawn out by the earlier salt.
Leave it uncovered for a week and then cut the pieces into 1cm cubes and store them in a brine solution of 7g of salt per litre.

Gorgonpaula Cheese

Gorgonzola, in Italy, is the only place where Gorgonzola can officially be made so I have called this after myself! Whether I look Gorgon-like is open to speculation. It is usually made from Ewe's milk but you can really use any milk for this.

Ingredients:

4.5 litres of fresh milk.
I litre of fresh double cream.
100ml of mesophilic starter culture.
Ig (an eighth of a teaspoon) of Penicillium roqueforti.
6 drops of rennet.
Cheese cloth.

Instructions:

Combine the milk, starter and Penicillium roqueforti, stirring well. Increase the temperature slowly to 28°C.
Leave them for 30 minutes at room temperature and then add the rennet in a small quantity of cooled, boiled water.
Leave the mix for 30 minutes, then cut the curds into I cm cubes.
Allow the curds to settle for 15 minutes, then carefully pour off the whey.
Form the cheese into plastic moulds and allow it to drain for a day in humid conditions, turning them every 8 hours.
Remove them from the mould, salt all the surfaces and leave to stand for two more days, salting the surfaces every time you turn them. This is done by lightly rubbing the surface with a large pinch of salt. In all, you will not use more than about 10g of salt for a cheese made from 4.5 litres of milk.
Pierce the cheese with a sterilised knitting needle from all directions so the Penicillium roqueforti can start to grow.
The cheese will be ready in a month.

Gouda Cheese

This hard cheese from Holland is cooked and brined like Parmesan but can be waxed, and is not aged for quite so long. In all other respects, they are very similar. The waxing is designed to stop any moisture loss.

Ingredients:

4.5 litres of milk.
100ml of mesophilic starter.
4 drops of rennet in cooled, boiled water.

Instructions:

Bring the milk to 29°C and mix in the starter thoroughly. Add the rennet and mix it well for five minutes. Keep it at a constant 29°C for up to 90 minutes.
Cut the curds into 1cm cubes, leaving them for ten minutes. Over an hour, raise the temperature to 39°C, gently stirring the curds to keep them separate.
Keep at this temperature for an hour. You will also need some boiled water at the same temperature. Remove around 600ml (say 3 cup fulls) of whey and replace them with the same amount of water at the same temperature. Every 15 or so minutes repeat this dilution of the whey. Drain the curds into a cheesecloth lined colander and then transfer them to a mould. Press, gradually increasing the pressure until it is heavily pressed. Keep at the top pressure for 3 hours.
Remove and float the cheese in medium cold brine (200g per litre of boiled water) for six hours, turning twice.
Pat it dry and set it to dry in the fridge for a month. Cover it with a basin after a week. Inspect it regularly for mould which can be wiped off with strong brine or vinegar. After a month the cheese can be waxed for storage.

Gruyere Cheese

A Swiss cheese that is so light it has holes in it. Well almost! It can be made from skimmed milk and certain recipes call for skimmed evening milk and non skimmed morning milk.

Ingredients:

4.5 litres of fresh milk.
100ml of thermophilic starter culture.
6 drops of rennet in a little cooled, boiled water.

Instructions:

Warm the milk to 32°C and add the starter, mixing well, and then leave it for 45 minutes.
Add the rennet and leave it until you get a clean break curd.
Over an hour, heat it to 52°C, stirring all the time with a whisk. You should get small, pea sized curds.
Drain the curds into cheesecloth lined moulds and press lightly for 12 hours.
Flip the cheese round and press lightly again for another 24 hours.
Float it in a light brine (200g per litre) for two days and then permit it to mature.
This maturing process is important!
Store it at around 10°C for the first week at 90% humidity and then at 20°C at 85% humidity for another five weeks.
Then store it at room temperature for another month.
The higher temperature causes gas to be formed in the cheese, hence the holes!

Guinness Cheese

This is basically the Cheshire cheese recipe with an approximation at making the amazingly savoury cheese you can buy at some food fairs and pubs.

Ingredients:

4.5 litres of milk.
100ml of mesophilic starter solution (buttermilk is good).
4 drops of rennet in a little cooled, boiled water.
Salt.
1 litre of Guinness (and another one for yourself).

Instructions:

Add the starter to the milk, slowly warm them to 29°C and then leave them for 30 minutes.
Add the rennet and leave for another 30 minutes to form the curd.
Cut the curds into 1cm cubes and increase the temperature to 35°C over about 30 minutes, then allow the curds to settle for 30 minutes.
Warm the Guinness in a pan until it is around 30°C and remove it from the heat. Add the curds and leave them for six hours.
Drain the curds into a colander lined with cheesecloth and, once drained, break up the curds into 1cm pieces and add 1% by weight of salt.
Place it into a mould lined with cheesecloth and press lightly overnight.
The following day, increase to full pressure and keep this up for 2 more days, opening and turning the cheese.

Put it to store, turningit every couple of days and the cheese will be ready in 3 weeks.

Halloumi Cheese

This is known as a Greek cheese although it was initially from Cyprus and was a traditional goat cheese. There are no starters involved.

Ingredients:

4.5 litres of resh milk, either goat, ewe or cow.
8 drops of rennet.
salt.
muslin.

Instructions:

Warm your milk to room temperature.
Leave it for an hour and when the curds have formed, ladel them into the cheesecloth in a colander.
Drain away any whey from the curds into a pan, and leave them to stand for half an hour as they firm up.
Meanwhile, bring the whey to the boil.
Place the curds into the boiling whey. and reduce the heat, then simmer until the cheese floats to the top.
Remove the cheese and cool it. Incorporate 1% salt by weight.
It is usually stored in a little whey in jars. Consequently, it needs to be stored cool.

Mascarpone Cheese

This is a simple cream cheese that will save you a fortune if you make your own.

Ingredients:

1 quart of double cream.
2g (a quarter of a teaspoon) of tartaric acid.

Instructions:

Slowly and carefully heat the cream to 80°C. Do not let it catch.
Add the tartaric acid and stir it for 10 minutes. Very fine curds should form. If not, add a pinch more (0.5 g) and stir for a further 10 minutes.
With a double layer of fine cheesecloth in a colander, carefully strain off the whey.
Leave it for 90 minutes to strain and then put the colander in the fridge overnight in a bowl to collect the drips.
The cheese is now ready and can be sweetened or eaten as required.

Melting Cheese

A raclette is a Swiss fondu, made by holding the cheese in front of the fire and allowing it to melt. The melted cheese is then scraped away. The name raclette means to scrape. So this is a recipe for a good melting cheese. You really do need a double boiler to warm the cheese slowly enough. The whole point of this cheese is that it is done slowly and gently.

Ingredients:

4.5 litres of fresh milk.
100ml of mesophilic starter culture.
6 drops of rennet in a little cooled, boiled water.

Instructions:

Warm the milk to 32°C and add the starter, mixing well and leave it to work for an hour.
Add the rennet and whisk it constantly for 5 minutes.
Allow the cheese to set for 1 hour and then cut the curds into 0.5cm cubes. Leave it to sit for 15 minutes.
Boil a kettle of water and allow it to cool to 50°C. Keep it ready for washing the curds.
Give the curds a stir and ladle away a measured amount, replacing it with the same amount of cooled boiled water at 50°C. Repeat this until the washing water has gone.
Allow the curds to rest for an hour, slowly removing the whey as you go.
Drain the curds into a cheesecloth lined colander.
Shape the cheese in the cloth and place it into a strong brine (330g per litre).
After six hours in the brine, flip the cheese over and give it another six hours. Repeat this step one more time.
Remove it and leave it to dry.

Mozzarella cheese

This cheese is kneaded to give it the correct consistency. It does not lose its fat under heat, making it ideal for pizzas.

Ingredients:

4.5 litres of milk.
75ml of buttermilk.
75ml of plain, natural yoghurt.
6 drops of rennet dissolved in cooled, boiled water.

Instructions:

Heat the milk in a double boiler to 32°C and maintain the heat. Add the yoghurt and buttermilk and stir vigorously to remove any lumps. Leave it for 15 minutes.
Add the rennet and mix well. Wait for 30 minutes and then cut the curds into 1cm cubes, all the while keeping the temperature constant. Allow the curds to settle for 15 minutes, stirring them gently with a clean hand.
Gently drain the curds into a muslin lined colander. The curds will form a single mass quite easily, which you should then wash in cold water.
Allow the curds to drain in the refrigerator overnight.
Next day, allow the curds to warm to room temperature. The culture will still be growing and the acidity of the curds will be increasing.
Cut yourself 3 1cm cubes.
Heat a pan of water to 72°C and immerse the cubes for 5 minutes. Then remove and try to mould them like plasticene. Reheat them in the pan for a minute and then try to pull them apart. If they break, wait another hour and retest them.
When it pulls like a rope the cheese is ready.
Cut all the cheese into small cubes and put them into a pan covered with water at 72°C. Allow the temperature to drop to around 55°C and squeeze the cubes together. Knead them by joining and stretching.
Form balls of cheese around 250g each (you should get 2 from 4.5 litres of milk).
Salt them for 5 hours in 7% brine.

Mrs Mehra's Paneer recipe

Paneer is a rubbery cheese, similar in texture to tofu. Bland on its own, it is a great ingredient in other dishes because it readily absorbs flavours.

Ingredients:

3 litres of whole milk.
200ml of natural yoghur.t
3/4 tablespoons of white vinegar.
Muslin cloth.

Instructions:

Gently warm all the milk and bring it slowly to the boil. As the milk begins to boil, lower the cooking heat and add the yoghurt and white vinegar, stirring gently to ensure that the vinegar disperses throughout the mixture. The curds will separate very quickly and as soon as they do, remove the pan from the heat.

Let the mixture cool and settle for approximately 10 minutes, giving it time to complete the coagulation and also time for the curd to harden.

Pour the curds and whey mix into a colander lined with a muslin cloth. This will drain off the whey through the muslin. When the whey (water) has drained off (after perhaps 10 minutes) gather the sides of the muslin cloth and tie it up, twisting gently to drain of any further whey.

Whilst still tied up in the muslin cloth, run the whey under a cold tap to remove the vinegar taste.

Lay this bundle of curds in the cloth on a chopping board and place something heavy on it, ensuring that the weight is even and fully covers the bundle. This will help any further whey to escape, and will help to harden the curd further.

For best results, leave the curds, now paneer, to set for 3 to 4 hours. Once set, remove the weight and slowly remove the muslin cloth. The slab of paneer is now ready to cut.

A heavy pan is rested on the cubes of paneer until they set hard. The cubes can be lightly fried until brown on all sides and are now ready to be added to your chosen curries or even salads etc.

Mysost Cheese

This Ricotta is a northern ricotta, in a way. You need a double boiler and the ability to hold the cheese at just below boiling point. It must be held at this temperature for a long time so you have to be very careful not to spoil it.

Ingredients:

1 litre of whole milk.
1 litre of whey.
400ml of double cream.

Instructions:

Combine the milk and the other ingredients.
Slowly heat the milk, being careful not to allow it to stick in the double boiler.
The simmering milk will not have any curds because the action of the simmer will mix it.
Watch the milk does not boil over or run dry; the simmer should be just at the simmer and held there.
Eventually the cheese mix will become fudge like and will darken in colour and set if taken from the heat.
Transfer it to a cheeseboard and shape it if required. You can use those new silicone moulds if you like.
The resulting cheeses are very sweet, due to a large amount of lactose.

Neufchatel Cheese

This is a French cheese from Normandy and is traditionally made from goat's milk. It can, however, be made from any milk and is a great substitute for cream cheese. This is made from whole milk, not cream.

Ingredients:

4.5 litres of fresh milk.
100ml of mesophilic starter culture.
8 drops of rennet.
Cheese cloth.

Instructions:

Combine the milk with the starter and leave them for an hour at room temperature.
Add the rennet to the milk in a small quantity of cooled, boiled water.
Cover and set them aside to set overnight at 20°C.
Ladle the curds into a colander lined with a fine cheesecloth.
Drain for around 8 hours, draw up the corners of the cloth and hang it.
Mix the curds by hand until they become a little like pasta.
Drain the curds and place them in a bowl.
Season them with a teaspoon of salt.

Parmesan cheese

This is a dried Italian cheese which is sprinkled or grated over minestrone soup and a million other dishes. It is salted and dried for a long time, consequently it is expensive to buy.

Ingredients:

4.5 litres of milk.
100ml of thermophilic starter solution.
6 drops of rennet in a small amount of cooled, boiled water.

Instructions:

Add the starter to the milk and slowly warm them to 40°C. Leave them for 1 hour at this temperature.
Take off the heat and five minutes later add the rennet and allow 45 minutes for the curds to form.
Carefully, but throughly, cut the curd into 0.5cm cubes.
Slowly, over an hour, increase the temperature to 52°C. During this heating, move the curds around a little to keep them separate. Keep them at this temperature for 45 minutes, by which time they should have become quite small and hardened.
Line a colander with cheesecloth and drain the curds. Transfer the curds to a mould and press lightly for an hour and then with medium pressure overnight.
Make a brine solution from 330g of salt in 1 litre of water and float the cheese in this for 2 days, turning it over every 8 - 10 hours or so. The outer skin should now be hardening. Pat it dry and leave it on a plate in the fridge, open to the air. After a week you can cover it with a dish.
Leave it for six months to mature and dry. If any mould forms, wipe it off with some strong brine or a little vinegar.

Queso Blanco Cheese

This is the South American version of paneer. There are many versions around the world, from China to, well, back round to China actually. It is cooked with and sometimes eaten raw.

Ingredients:

4.5 litres of whole milk.
The juice of 4 lemons.

Instructions:

Heat the milk until it is at 82°C. You will need to stir it so as not to burn the milk and maintain the temperature as closely as possible.
Continue to stir and slowly add the lemon juice. Leave it for 15 minutes. If no curds form, add more lemon juice.
Line a colander with muslin and filter the curds.
Allow them to settle and cool for 30 minutes.
Tie the muslin and hang it for as long as necessar to remove the whey.
Salt to 1% by weight and break up the curds and reform it.

Queso Fresco cheese

This is another South American cheese which is similar to Queso Blanco but requires rennet. It uses buttermilk and fresh milk in equal proportions.

Ingredients:

4.5 litres of buttermilk and whole milk mixed 50:50.
4 drops of rennet in a little cooled, boiled water.
Muslin.

Instructions:

Mix your milk and allow it to attain room temperature.
Slowly heat it to 34°C.
Add the rennet and mix it well.
Leave it for 30 minutes, then cut the curd into 2cm cubes.
Raise the temperature to 40°C and leave the curds for 10 minutes.
Allow the curds to stand for 15 minutes and drain them into a colander lined with a cheesecloth.
Twist the cheesecloth so the curds form a ball and squeeze the whey out.
Break the curds and add 1% of salt by weight - this will bring out more whey, which can be squeezed to remove it as before.
Roll the cheese into a ball and store it in the fridge.

Really Quick Cheshire

Or should this be creamy Lancashire? I don't know because, to be honest, I can hardly tell the difference. This is really quick and easy to do and there is no storage. You could store it and I am sure it would improve, but we are just hungry and greedy people and we have never been able to get round to maturing it.

Ingredients:

4.5 litres of milk.
1 pot of creme fraiche (450ml).
6 drops of rennett in a little cooled, boiled water.

Instructions:

Warm the milk to 30°C and add the creme fraiche. Turn the heat off and leave it for 30 minutes (or as long as it takes to make and drink a cup of tea).
Add the rennet and leave it for another hour.
Cut the curds into 1cm cubes and pour them into a cheesecloth lined colander.
Salt to 1% by weight and mix it well by hand.
Squeeze out the rest of the whey and transfer the cheese to a mould in the muslin.
Press it gradually, increasing to medium weight for the rest of the day.
Empty the cheese out onto a plate and eat it!

Ricotta # 1

This Ricotta is basically acidified milk heated to a high but carefully controlled temperature. The caesin curds form because of the acid and the albuminous curds form because of the temperature. The two curds are collected together.

You have to be careful not to loose the curds through the cheesecloth.

Ingredients:

4.5 litres of milk.
The juice of 4 lemons.
Some salt.

Instructions:

Combine the milk and lemon juice.
Slowly heat the milk, being careful not to scald it on the sides of the pan.
At 83°C the curds will rise to the surface.
Leave the milk at this temperature for 5 minutes and then ladle them into prepared cheesecloths.
The cheesecloth are dampened and folded to make 5 or 6 layers. Use only the finest muslin.
Carefully ladle the curds onto the cheesecloths and pull the corners together to hand.
Allow it to drain in the fridge, for 4 hours, if possible.
Carefully salt it to 1% by weight and store in the fridge.

Add some garlic and olive oil to ricotta and it is frequently used for ravioli recipes.

Ricotta # 2

This is a whey made ricotta. It calls for a gallon of fresh whey, so you will have already made cheese from 2 gallons of milk in order to get enough to use. You can freeze whey but the process is not so good. You really do need fresh whey if it is available.

Ingredients:

1 litre of whole milk.
4.5 litres of whey.
The juice of 5 lemons (or 50ml white wine vinegar)

Instructions:
Combine the milk and whey and heat them to 92°C.
Remove them from the heat and add the acid, stirring gently.
Pour it into a fine cheesecloth in a colander and allow it to drain.
Tie up the corners and allow it to drip for 4 hours or until the cheese has stopped dripping completely.

You can add some cream or buttermilk to alter the consistency and you can add any number of flavours you choose.

Romano cheese

This is like Parmesan but less so. Everything in it is done to a lesser degree but the same processes are at work. This cheese is at least 2000 years old (the recipe, not the maturing time).

Ingredients:

4.5 litres of milk.
100ml of thermophilic starter solution.
6 drops of rennet in a small amount of cooled, boiled water.

Instructions:

Add the starter to the milk and slowly warm them to 32°C. Leave for 30 minutes at this temperature.
Take off the heat and, five minutes later, add the rennet and allow 45 minutes for the curds to form.
Carefully, but throughly, cut the curd into 0.5cm cubes.
Slowly, over an hour, increase the temperature to 46°C. During this heating, move the curds around a little to keep them separate. Keep at this temperature for 45 minutes.
Line a colander with cheesecloth and drain the curds.
Transfer the curds to a mould and press lightly for an hour and then hard overnight.
Remove the cheese and pit it - that is prick the surface with a sterile knitting needle or fork so it looks a bit like the surface of a golf ball.
Make a brine solution from 200g of salt in 1 litre of water and float the cheese in this for 12 hours.
Pat it dry and leave it open to the air on a plate in the fridge. After a week you can coverit with a dish.

Leave it for six months to mature and dry. If any mould forms, wipe it off with some strong brine or a little vinegar.

Roule cheese

This is one of those prepared cheeses that we can only approximate, but it is great fun and gives fantastic results. I have used here the basic recipe for Queso Fresco, but this also works particularly well with basic goat's cheese.

Ingredients:

4.5 litres of buttermilk and whole milk mixed 50:50.
4 drops of rennet in a little cooled, boiled water.
Muslin and cling film.
2 bulbs of garlic.
Chopped herbs (chives, parsley or sage or all!).
Cracked pepper corns.

Instructions:

Mix your milk and allow it to attain room temperature.
Slowly heat to 34°C.
Add the rennet and mix well.
Leave it for 30 minutes then cut the curd into 2cm cubes.
Drain it into a colander lined with a cheesecloth.
Twist the cheesecloth so that the curds form a ball and squeeze the whey out.
Break the curds and add 1% of salt by weight then squeeze out more whey as before.
Put into a dish and fork in some cream to make a light paste..
Crush and paste your garlic and chop up your herbs.
Combine the cheese, garlic and herbs.
Spoon out the cheese onto a piece of cling film (wet muslin will do) and then sprinkle the surface with crushed peppercorn so it forms a dark layer.
Carefully roll the cheese like a Swiss roll. Slice and store it covered in the fridge.

Saint Maure

This is a form of Chevre using Penicillium candidum in the starter. This oozes quite quickly and unless you do not want to have to chase your cheese down the street, eat it after a couple of weeks. You will find that the cheese becomes furry quite easily. Watch out for any blueness. If discovered the cheese should be discarded.

Ingredients:

4.5 litres of goat's milk.
4 drops of rennet in a little cooled, boiled water.
1g of Penicillium candidum (an eighth of a teaspoon).
1 pot (200 ml) of buttermilk.

Instructions:

Heat the milk to 26°C . Add the buttermilk and the Penicillium candidum and wait for 30 mins.
Add the rennet and wait for 30 minutes, then cut the curds into 1cm cubes.
Drain them into a cheesecloth lined colander and hang for six hours. Squeeze them into a ball shape and run off the excess whey.
Lightly press them into a mould for ten minutes and remove to sprinkle all the outer edges with salt.
Leave it on a plate covered with a dish in the fridge for a week and eat it the following week. You can wipe the furriness if you like.

Smoked Cheese

Using something like Edam as a base, you can make smoked cheese that is so much better than the processed stuff you buy in the shops. American smoked cheese is impossible to recreate without a factory, so we haven't even tried.

We have missed out the cheese bit of the recipe here because you can smoke anything. The knack is in knowing your smoker and how to control its temperature of delivery exactly. You should aim to smoke at no higher that 22°C and the smoking time should be slow. Large cheeses, larger than the recipes in this book, of two kilos and over should be smoked for at least 24 hours. Smaller cheeses, of 500g, the approximate amount of cheese delivered from our recipes as they are, should be smoked for 8 hours.

You can smoke at any one of two points but if you are looking to make a speciality cheese that is well smoked to the centre, try smoking the curds at the milling point when you have broken them up and added salt, just before smoking.

You have to remember that the smoking process will increase the drying of the cheese and with this in mind it is good for cheeses that are a little moist. You have to be careful not to try to smoke everything. For myself, something like a smoked Brie would be unpleasant in the extreme.

Do not smoke with pine or any resinous wood, but use good quality hardwoods, oak probably being the best bet, but both apple and cherry are good too.

Spreadable Goat's Cheese

This cheese is simple to make and should serve as a template for all goat cheeses.

Ingredients:

2 litres of fresh goat's milk.
25ml of mesophilic starter culture.
1 drop of rennet in a little cooled, boiled water.
2.5g of salt.

Instructions:

Slowly warm the milk to 21°C using a double boiler if at all possible.
Add the starter, mixing well and then, ten minutes later, add the rennet.
Leave it for at least 12 hours to set.
Carefully ladle out the curds and let them drain for 24 hours.
The cheese should have a firmness about it.
You can incorporate salt and herbs at this stage if you wish.
Rolling the cheeses into chopped herbs makes a great presentation feature.

Wensleydale Cheese

This was initially a ewe's milk cheese. The great Abbeys of Yorkshire owned most of the North of England and, of course, the tenant farmers that lived on them. It was here that this cheese was first made. It is now made from cow's milk. You can get both white and blue types.

Ingredients:

4.5 litres of really creamy milk.
100ml of mesophilic starter culture.
1g (an eighth of a teaspoon) of Penicillium roqueforti.
4 drops of rennet in a little cooled, boiled water.
Salt.

Instructions:

Mix the milk, the Penicillium roqueforti and the starter and heat them to 30°C.
Add the rennet and wait for an hour for it to set.
Cut the curds into 2cm cubes and allowthem to rest for 30 minutes and, in that time, raise the temperature to 33°C.
Pour them into a cheesecloth lined colander and drain them for 20 minutes.
Re-cut the curd into 1cm cubes and drain off further whey.
Salt at 2% by weight.
Put the curds into a lined mould and press lightly overnight.
Bandage or wax the cheese and ripen it for a month.
I have found that waxed blue Wensledale does not do so well wrapped at first and I have resorted to piercing the cheese like any other blue.

If you want white Wensledale, simply miss out the culture of Penicillium Roqueforti.

White Stilton Cheese

This is approximated in a number of recipes, both on the internet and in books and, frankly, they do not seem to be that good. This one is the nearest I have found and is, in a way, a mixture of both cheddar and blue Stilton.

Ingredients:

4.5 litres of really creamy milk.
1 litre of double cream.
100ml of mesophilic starter culture.
8 drops of rennet in a little cooled, boiled water.
5g of salt.

Instructions:

Mix the milk and cream and heat them to 33°C.
Add the culture and rennet and wait for 90 minutes at a constant temperature.
Cut the curds into 1cm cubes and allowthem to rest for 30 minutes.
Pour them into a cheesecloth lined colander and drain for 20 minutes.
Cut the cheese into blocks of around 10cm square and stack them. Reorder the stacks every 30 minutes for 90 minutes. The acidity will have built up inside the curds.
Break up the curds and evenly mix in the salt.
Spoon the curds into a 10cm mould and allow them to settle, forcing the cheese down with a spoon. Repeatedly turn the mould upside down until the cheese falls under its own weight. Keep the outside moist and allow the cheese to slip out of the mould once it has shrunk.
Ripen the cheese in a sterile, sealable plastic box at room temperature for a week and then pop it into the fridge to continue for a couple more weeks.

Glossary

Acid
This is the amount of hydrogen ions in the whey. This comes mostly from lactic acid and is produced by bacteria. It is measured with a pH meter or strips of indicator paper that change colour and you read off the acidity against a chart.

Aging
The process of allowing a cheese to mature once it has been formed. This has to be done in clean conditions. Some cheeses require no aging while others may need a year.

Albumenous protein
Rather than just calling it albumen, the same as an egg white, this protein is mammalian in origin (obviously). It is precipitated out of the whey by heat, just like boiling an egg, I suppose. It is used to make cheeses like ricotta.

Annatto
All cheese (well more or less) would be white unless it was dyed. Annatto is a vegetable dye and a few drops are needed to colour the whole batch.

Antibiotics
Substances from Penicillium and other fungi that inhibit the growth of bacteria. In milk you might find that the cheese will not curd because the acidity is too low.

Bacteria
Life forms that mostly produce their energy without oxygen and their waste product is lactic acid. The acid makes the cheese curdle. Some bacteria, known as pathogens, are dangerous to human health. You need to be sure you are growing only the right ones. Usually the smell is a good indication of suitability, but not in the case of Lysteria. Use Pasteurised milk and keep

everything sterile.

Bag cheese
This is a cheese that gets its shape from the cheesecloth as it hangs. A kind of ball – like a mozzarella.

Bloom
This is the name for the fungus spore bodies that make a colour or furr on the cheese.

Brine
A salt solution. This helps to form a rind on a cheese which then holds the rest of the cheese in place while it ripens. It is often a saturated salt solution which is made by heating a litre of water and dissolving 350g of salt into it. This is then slowly cooled to stop crystals coming out of the solution.

Casein
This is the protein in milk that is coagulated by rennet or acid.

Cheddaring
The cutting of curds into strips that are then stored, one on top of another and are sometimes turned or rotated, prior to salting and the rest of the cheese making process.

Cheesecloth
A cotton sheet that is coarsely woven but strong enough to hold curds and drain whey. It does not easily clog up and will boil easily to sterilise.

Citrate and citric acid
This is formed in citrus fruits, mostly lemons, and is used to make non-rennet cheeses or in the acidification process. It is implicated in the suckling of bad tempered people.

Clean cut
Push your finger into the curd. If it breaks in a clean cut then it is ready. It is a crack line, well defined and obviously different from a mushy mess of half set curds.

Culture
The name given to a living mass of bacteria or fungi growing in its food source.

Curd
The results of the first stage of cheesemaking, forming a semi-hard coagulated set in milk.

Emulsion
Milk is an emulsion; a mixture of suspended solids that are held in position by the action of the molecules around them. They do not separate.

Enzymes
The catalysts of chain reactions that promote metabolic processes. An enzyme will help to turn one substance into another without being used up itself. This is why so small an amount of rennet will curdle a lot of milk. The rennet is left to do its job again and again.

Follower
Can be either a plate that sits behind the plunger on the mould or a block that improves the reach of the press for higher pressing forces.

Foot
In a Brie you get a final rind towards the bottom of the cheese that can be more bitter than the cheese contents. It's a French way of being snobby about cheese because, on the whole, the cheese is cut through anyway.

Homogenised
Full milk that has been vibrated to force the cream on the top into the milk. Yum!

Inoculation
The act of purposely introducing bacteria into a substrate (milk). The inoculation of bacteria without knowing about it should be avoided.

Lactic acid
The product of anaerobic respiration (without oxygen) in bacteria. It increases the acidity of the milk.

Lactose
Milk sugarIt is converted into glucose by the bacteria in the starter.

Maturing
Keeping a cheese for a set number of days to improve its flavour or consistency.

Mastitis
An inflamation of the teat or the udder, often causing a blockage and resulting in blood in the milk.

Mesophilic
This term refers to a starter culture that does not grow when too hot, usually above 40°C. It prefers lower, luke warm temperatures.

Milling
Heating the curds and breaking them into smaller pieces.

Mould
This word has two meanings: the plastic circular mould that

the curds are pressed into or are set into to make the shape of the cheese. or it is another way of referring to any form of fungus such as Penicillium etc.

Needling
Piercing a cheese which has Penicillium roqueforti in the culture in order to introduce air that will trigger the mould to produce the blue colour and the tangy flavour.

Pasteurise
Milk heated to a temperature that kills most of the bacteria but does not alter the flavour. In particular, Lysteria is killed. Some people believe Lysteria is an important part of some cheeses, but it can cause troublesome and even dangerous disease symptoms.

Pathogen
A bacteria or microbe that will cause human disease.

Pasty
An overly dry cheese

Penicillium
A whole series of fungi useful in cheese making, particularly Brie and Camembert.

pH
The measure of acidity, or the hydrogen ion concentration.

Pitch
Allowing curds to rest in whey, often for cooking purposes.

Pressing
Forcing whey out of curds under pressure and making a specific shape.

Rennet
The enzyme that coagulates casein and is made from rennin, the enzyme found in the young ruminant's stomach. You can buy vegetarian rennet made from various plants and algae.

Ropey
Milk from a badly infected udder. It has coagulated protein and sometimes contains blood. All udders contain bacteria, but enzymes keep the milk from spoiling unless there is a bacterial overload.

Salting
Adding salt, usually to the rate of 1% of the final weight of a cheese. Salt is not used to preserve cheese in the same way as for meat. Cheese is usually a biological ecosystem where pathogen bacteria are 'outgrown' by the ones with which we inoculate the cheese.

Scalding
Also known as cooking the curd. It is a reference to increasing the temperature of the mix so the curds lose more whey and become smaller.

Starter
A culture of bacteria in milk that is used to increase the acidity of the milk and add a ripened flavour.

Taint
Any flavour that has been passed to the milk in an unplanned way. Garlic and onion are favourites.

Thermophilic
Refers to a starter culture that will work at a higher temperature in excess of 42°C and used frequently in the production of hard cheeses.

Wax
A red, black, yellow, green or orange wax used specially for coating cheese.

Whey
The liquid left behind when the curds have been removed. Whey is still full of nutrients and should not be considered as waste material. Feed it to the pigs, make cakes or even make more cheese with it – ricotta for example.

Finally I leave you with this thought:

"The early bird may get the worm, but it is the second mouse that gets the cheese."

Resources

Getting started:

Ascott Smallholding Supplies
The Old Creamery
Four Crosses
Llanymynech
Powys
SY22 6LP
Telephone: 0845 130 6285
www.ascott.biz

Moorlands Cheesemakers
Brewhamfield Farm
North Brewham
Bruton
Somerset
BA10 0QQ
Telephone: 01749 850108
www.cheesemaking.co.uk

Smallholder Supplies
The Old Post Office
6 Main Street
Branston
Nr. Grantham
Lincs
NG 32 1RU
Telephone: 01476 870070
www.smallholdersupplies.co.uk

National Associations:

The British Cheese Board
29 – 35 Lexington Street
London
W1F 9AH
Telephone: 0117 9211744
enquiries@britishcheese.com

The British Sheep Dairying Association
The Estate Office
Torry Hill
Milstead
Sittingbourne
Kent
ME9 0SP
Telephone: 01795 830100
www.sheepdairying.com

Foodlinks UK
c/o Envolve
Green Park Station
Bath
BA1 1JB
Telephone: 01225 787921
www.foodlinks-uk.org

The Guild of Fine Food
House Station Road
Wincanton
Somerset
BA9 9FE.
Telephone: 01963 824464
www.finefoodworld.co.uk

Periodicals

Artisan Magazine
Country Kitchen
Country Smallholding
Delicous
Farmers Guardian
Farmers Weekly
Grow It!
Smallholder
The Fine Food Digest.

Herbs

Designasausage
133 London Road
Macclesfield
SK11 7RL
Telephone: 08452 578884
www.designasausage.com

Weschenfelder
2 – 4 North Road
Middlesborough
Cleveland
TS2 1DE
Telephone: 01642 247524
www.weschenfelder.co.uk

Courses:

A B Cheesemaking
7 Daybell Close
Bottesford
Nottingham
NG13 0DQ
Telephone: 01949 842867
www.abcheesemaking.co.uk

The Guild of Fine Food
House Station Road
Wincanton
Somerset
BA9 9FE
Telephone: 01963 824464
www.finefoodworld.co.uk

The Guild runs training courses on cheese making for members.

Kitchenware:

Crocks and Pots
Challock
Nr Ashford
Kent
TN25 4DG
Telephone: 01233 740529
www.crocksandpots.com

Farmers Markets:

The National Association of Farmers Markets
Telephone: 0845 45 88 420
www.farmersmarkets.net

Country Markets:
Telephone: 01246 261508
www.country-markets.co.uk

Farmers Retail and Markets Association (FARMA)
12 Southgate Street
Winchester
SO23 9EF
Telephone: 0845 4588420
www.farma.org.uk

Cheese Shows:

The Nantwich International Cheese Show
c/o The Woodlands
Aston
Nantwich
CW5 8DB
Telephone: 01270 780306
www.nantwichshow.co.uk

The Frome Cheese Show
The Show Office
Rodden Road
Frome
Somerset
BA11 2AH
Telephone: 01373 463600
www.fromecheeseshow.co.uk

The Speciality Fine Food Fairs
The Guild of Fine Food
House Station Road
Wincanton
Somerset
BA9 9FE.
Telephone: 01963 824464
www.finefoodworld.co.uk

Held annually at Harrogate, Edinburgh and London and
run by The Guild of Fine Foods.

The Good Life Press Ltd., is a family run specialist publisher and retailer catering for the farmer, smallholder and the specialist food producer.

Other titles by the same author and published by the imprint, Farming Books and Videos, are:-

The Sausage Book
The Smoking and Curing Book
Jack Hargreaves - A Portrait
A Good Life
How to Butcher Livestock and Game

The Wild Food Book is due out in 2008

Other titles of interest published by us are:

A Guide to Traditional Pig Keeping
Traditional Cattle Breeds
An Introduction to Keeping Sheep

Farming Books and Videos
PO Box 536
Preston
PR2 9ZY
www.farmingbooksandvideos.com
www.thegoodlifepress.co.uk